Living
the
Proverbs

Insight *for the* Daily Grind

Living
the
Proverbs

Insight *for the* Daily Grind

CHARLES R.
SWINDOLL

WORTHY®
PUBLISHING

Published by Worthy Books, an imprint of Worthy Publishing Group, a division of Worthy Media, Inc., One Franklin Park, 6100 Tower Circle, Suite 210, Franklin, TN 37067.

WORTHY is a registered trademark of Worthy Media, Inc.

HELPING PEOPLE EXPERIENCE THE HEART OF GOD

eBook available at www.worthypublishing.com

Library of Congress Control Number: 2012949762

The content of this book was derived from the previously published Living Beyond the Daily Grind, Books I and II.

All Scripture quotations, unless otherwise indicated, are taken from the New American Standard Bible®. Copyright © 1960, 1962, 1963, 1968, 1971, 1972, 1973, 1975, 1977, 1995. The Lockman Foundation. Used by permission.

Scripture quotations marked KJV are taken from the King James Version.

Scripture quotations marked TLB are taken from the Living Bible.

For foreign and subsidiary rights, contact rights@worthypublishing.com

Published in association with Yates & Yates, www.yates2.com

ISBN: 978-1-93603-471-0 (hardcover w/ jacket)
ISBN: 978-1-61795-373-6 (trade paper)

Cover Design: Christopher Tobias, Tobias' Outerwear for Books
Cover Image: Mark Owen/arcangel-images.com
Interior Design and Typesetting: Kimberly Sagmiller, Fudge Creative

Printed in the United States of America
17 18 19 20 VPI 8 7 6 5 4

CONTENTS

INTRODUCTION

Here is more good news for those who are struggling to live beyond the grinding hassles of everyday life. This volume journeys through selections from the book of Proverbs, applying the soothing oil of these wise words from Israel's sages to such daily challenges as imbalance, addiction, sorrow, excuse-making, envy, financial problems, motherhood, and numerous other issues and struggles.

My approach in this volume will be the same as in *Living the Psalms*—practical and relevant rather than analytical and scholarly. From my more than five decades in ministry, I have learned that the quickest way to put the truth of Scripture into people's lives is both through their heart and through their head. This is especially true of the Proverbs. God has preserved these wise sayings not simply for the purpose of intellectual stimulation but for their practical application as well. If we are ever going to put biblical principles into action, we must deliberately resist the temptation to substitute analysis for appropriation.

This is not to say that we should drift and dream our way through Scripture, spiritualizing this phrase or that, hoping that a few ideas will inadvertently lodge in our minds like floating sticks snagged on a river bank. On the contrary, God's Book deserves our serious concentration as we seek to apply its wisdom to the nagging and inescapable pressures with which we live. At the same time, however, we must not miss the beauty of its poetry as we pursue the practicality of its message. Keeping this balance can be tricky. In one of his lesser known works, *Reflections on the Psalms*, C. S. Lewis addresses the need for this balance that I am attempting to describe. I could not agree more with his observations:

In this book, then, I write as one amateur to another, talking about difficulties I have met, or lights I have gained, when reading the Psalms, with the hope that this might at any rate interest, and sometimes even help, other inexpert readers. I am "comparing notes," not presuming to instruct.

We will strive to maintain such a delicate balance in our study of Proverbs: appreciating its poetry while still reflecting meaningfully on its application for us today. I will also continue in this book the same approach I took with *Living the Psalms*. We will examine a specific topic for one week, which will be broken down into daily readings, each of which culminates in a point of reflection and application.

Before getting underway, I must pause and express my gratitude to Byron Williamson of Worthy Publishing. Byron has been far more than a business associate in the publishing industry. He is a true friend whose sincere affirmation fuels my fire. Along with him I thank Mark Gaither, my son-in-law, who is also my excellent editor. His careful attention to detail has been of inestimable value and my gratitude knows no bounds. And I also want to mention Sealy Yates, my longtime friend and literary agent, who has no equal in diligence or in commitment.

Words fail me as I attempt to describe the depth of my gratitude to my wife for her understanding, unselfishness, and encouragement. Without her willingness to adapt to my writing schedule; to listen patiently to my incessant reading of what I have written; to prod me on during the dry spells; and to tolerate the late-night, middle-of-the-night, and early-morning flashes of insight that kept the light burning over the desk in my home study—there is no way I could have reached this milestone.

And now . . . let's press on. The year stretches out in front of us, and God's wisdom awaits our appropriation. I commend you for your faithful diligence. There are many who graze through the Bible, randomly nibbling here and yon with only a passing interest in the words on a page. Few are those who drink deeply and consistently from the streams of living water. May our Lord richly reward you for your commitment and diligence to learning and living His truth. Ultimately, may He use these pages to help you live beyond the daily grind.

Chuck Swindoll
Frisco, Texas

THE GRIND OF HUMAN VIEWPOINT

The proverbs of Solomon the son of David, king of Israel:
To know wisdom and instruction,
To discern the sayings of understanding,
To receive instruction in wise behavior,
Righteousness, justice and equity;
To give prudence to the naive,
To the youth knowledge and discretion,
A wise man will hear and increase in learning,
And a man of understanding will acquire wise counsel,
To understand a proverb and a figure,
The words of the wise and their riddles.

The fear of the LORD is the beginning of knowledge;
Fools despise wisdom and instruction.

Hear, my son, your father's instruction
And do not forsake your mother's teaching;
Indeed, they are a graceful wreath to your head
And ornaments about your neck.

(Proverbs 1:1–9)

Day 1: *Proverbs 1*
Life in Three Dimensions

Every waking moment of our lives, we operate from one of two viewpoints: human or divine. I sometimes refer to these as the horizontal perspective and the vertical perspective. Humanity remains willfully and stubbornly limited to the horizontal. We jealously guard our autonomy from heaven: we much prefer to think, maintain our attitudes, and conduct our lives independent of our Maker. Consequently, human opinions influence us more than God's commands and principles. We base our choices on what's best for ourselves and our loved ones (maybe) without much regard for the long-term moral implications. Horizontal solutions give us the illusion of greater security and pleasure, so we tend to either reject or ignore vertical remedies to our challenges. For example, when under the gun of some deadline, we desperately search for a tangible way out rather than heed God's counsel to trust Him. Instead of waiting on our Lord to solve our dilemma in His own way and in His own time, we usually step in and begin manipulating a quick, painless escape.

Because divine wisdom fills the book of Proverbs, we can anticipate a vertical perspective even though the grind of having a strictly human viewpoint comes so naturally. This vertical wisdom includes practical guidance to help us live wisely in the horizontal dimension. Therefore, the more we pore over the sayings in Scripture, the more oil we apply to the daily grind. Without a doubt, the wisdom of Solomon and other Hebrew sages offers the most practical, down-to-earth instruction in all the Bible. The entire book of thirty-one chapters is filled with capsules of truth, often in the form of a short, pithy maxim, to help us face and even rise above the daily grinds of life. These sayings convey specific truth in such a pointed and easy-to-understand manner that we will have little difficulty grasping the message.

Reflections

Think of a significant decision you made in the past. What additional insight emerged when you considered that situation from the vertical perspective? Considering the outcome with the benefit of hindsight, what impact did the vertical perspective have on your decision—and having done that . . . what, if anything, would you do differently?

Day 2: *Proverbs 1*

Wisdom and Style

The book of Proverbs conveys divine wisdom—practical counsel with a vertical dimension—in a style that follows the conventions of Hebrew poetry. The most common structure in Proverbs, for instance, is the couplet. The writer places two ideas side by side such that each complements the other. Take Proverbs 13:10, for example:

> Through insolence comes nothing but strife,
> But wisdom is with those who receive counsel.

The book of Proverbs employs at least four distinct types of couplet: contrastive, completive, corresponding, and comparative.

In a contrastive couplet, the key term is usually *but*. One statement contrasts with the other to show two sides of the same coin, as it were. The contrasting conjunction links the statements together, yet keeps the two ideas distinct. Each statement can stand alone but, together, their message becomes more profound.

> A wise son accepts his father's discipline,
> But a scoffer does not listen to rebuke. (13:1)

> Poverty and shame will come to him who neglects discipline,
> But he who regards reproof will be honored. (13:18)

> He who withholds his rod hates his son,
> But he who loves him disciplines him diligently. (13:24)

In completive couplets, the second statement completes the first. The first statement, while true in itself, doesn't offer a complete picture without the second. These couplets typically feature coordinating conjunctions like *and* or *so*.

> The heart knows its own bitterness,
> And a stranger does not share its joy. (14:10)

> Even in laughter the heart may be in pain,
> And the end of joy may be grief. (14:13)

> Commit your works to the LORD
> And your plans will be established. (16:3)

The corresponding couplet—very common in the Psalms as well—features two lines expressing the same thought using different terms. Another name for this kind of couplet is "synonymous parallelism." While the first statement expresses a complete idea, the second adds depth, dimension, and color. The effect is not unlike seeing the world through two eyes instead of just one. A person with one eye can observe the world, but he or she lacks depth perception. Two eyes allow us to perceive the world in 3D, which is so much better.

> The fear of the LORD is the beginning of wisdom,
> And the knowledge of the Holy One is understanding. (9:10)

The parallelism allows us to define the terms more precisely. "Fear of the Lord" and "knowledge of the Holy One" correspond to one another. To "fear" God, then, is to "know" Him—and vice versa. Moreover, "beginning of wisdom" and "understanding" correspond. They aren't exactly the same, but they share a common source: an intimate, in-depth relationship with God.

Finally, as the name *comparative couplets* suggests, the two statements invite a comparison. These feature terms like *better . . . than, as . . . so,* or *like . . . so.* For example:

> *Better* is a little with the fear of the LORD
> *Than* great treasure and turmoil with it. (15:16)

> It is *better* to live in a corner of the roof
> *Than* in a house shared with a contentious woman. (25:24)

Comparative sayings usually paint vivid word pictures that draw upon the reader's own experience to describe a new truth. The structure of the couplet implies, in effect, "This new truth is much like this other truth you already accept." Consequently, the word picture rings so true to life that the reader unconsciously nods in hearty agreement.

The style of Hebrew wisdom literature and other poetic expression isn't difficult to interpret, but it is somewhat different from our twenty-first-century Western writing. In what ways, if any, do you think this difference will affect your willingness to study the book of Proverbs? What does your willingness say about your desire for wisdom?

Day 3: *Proverbs 1*

True Wisdom

While much of the book of Proverbs came directly from the pen of Solomon, the finished work actually combines the wisdom of several sages, which a final editor compiled and arranged as we have it today. Ultimately, this is the work of the Holy Spirit. Like the sixty-six books of the Bible, Proverbs combines the writings of many human authors working under God's direct inspiration. Providence brought all the written material together through the efforts of an inspired compiler. This book of divine wisdom cannot be said to come from one individual; it truly is the mind of God expressed in writing.

After a brief preface (1:1–7), Proverbs can be divided into seven sections or collections:

The Words of Solomon on the Value of Wisdom (1:8–9:18)

The Proverbs of Solomon (10:1–22:16)

The Proverbs of Wise Men (22:17–24:34)

The Proverbs of Solomon Collected by Hezekiah's Men (25:1–29:27)

The Wisdom of Agur (30:1–33)

The Wisdom of Lemuel (31:1–31)

Unlike other books of the Bible, Proverbs contains no direct information about the people to whom it was originally written. It doesn't mention the Hebrew nation, its culture, customs, laws, or history. The Old Testament books of law and history require us to draw timeless principles from words written to people living far away and long ago; the book of Proverbs, however, is timeless and universal. The wisdom of Solomon and the other sages requires no translation; the truths apply to all people living everywhere at any time. Even so, we must consciously exchange our twenty-first-century Western filter for the worldview of the Hebrew God.

Western thinkers, for example, make a distinction between theoretical and practical wisdom; the Hebrew sages did not. In other words, Greek or Western philosophy teaches that a person can be filled with knowledge yet behave foolishly. Consequently, Western thinkers believe that our challenge is to live out what we say we believe to be true. Western philosophers call us to live up to our potential by putting into practice what we know to be true.

The Hebrew sages considered this nonsense. For a person to know truth and then behave contrary to that truth is the very definition of stupid! For example, if people accept the law of gravity as a fact and truly understand how it operates, we don't dance on the ledge of a skyscraper. If we do, our theoretical knowledge of gravity only makes us greater fools. Wise people stand clear of dangerous places and usually live longer as a result. In the Hebrew mind, to "know wisdom and instruction" necessarily means to put it into practice. Wisdom occurs when knowledge produces obedience.

As we read the wisdom of these Hebrew sages, we are wise to challenge many of the notions we take for granted. Rather than subject Proverbs to our preexisting opinions of what is right or wrong, good or bad, we must give this book the benefit of divine authority. That is to say, if we read these words with an open heart, we will find ourselves agreeing with what we read much of the time—and occasionally offended. When these words of divine wisdom cause inner turmoil, I urge you to pause. Don't dismiss it too quickly. This is your opportunity to allow the Holy Spirit to straighten out some faulty thinking and to set you on a corrected course. If you allow the Word of God and the Spirit of God complete access to your mind, then your life at home, at work, with friends, and in the world at large will be transformed. After all, the core message of the book of Proverbs is this: "Do things God's way, and you'll be more successful in every sphere of life. Ignore divine wisdom, and you will fail."

Reflections

Our Western mind-set tends to equate knowledge with wisdom. According to the Bible, people can be called "wise" only when they *behave* wisely. Education and insight aside, does your behavior reflect wisdom? Ask a trusted friend or mentor to answer that question for you.

Day 4: *Proverbs 1*
This Means You

While we are getting better acquainted with the ancient sayings, I should mention that this is a book full of various kinds of people facing a variety of common challenges. Years ago I completed an in-depth analysis of Proverbs and was surprised to discover that the book includes more than 180 types or categories of people. Men and women, young and old, foolish and wise, Jew and Gentile, rich and poor, married and single—Proverbs addresses virtually every demographic imaginable to offer specific advice concerning the issues they face. Moreover, the sages discuss circumstances that all people must face, regardless of age, gender, race, nationality, where they live, in what era, or even what religion they practice. Common themes include work, money, marriage, friendship, family, home life, hardships, conflict, youth, old age, sin, forgiveness . . . challenges for which everyone needs guidance. It's no wonder so many people throughout history have discovered this book to be helpful: when it comes to gaining wise counsel for horizontal living!

Despite the broad range of topics, however, everything eventually goes back to an individual's personal relationship with God and His Word. By the end of this book of wisdom, we discover a great paradox. Regardless of the categories that divide us, we human beings are united by the same challenges. Furthermore, the practical wisdom provided by the book of Proverbs points all people—our differences notwithstanding—in the same direction: toward a right relationship with God.

While the sages affirm a sole Deity ruling over humanity, they nevertheless present Him as a complex being with many facets to His personality and several roles to fill. He is transcendent (distinct from creation) yet immanent (personally involved within the world). He is the sovereign King of the universe, ineffable and inscrutable, yet He calls all people to a personal relationship with Him. He is the righteous judge, handing out rewards and punishments according to merit, yet He is the advocate of the helpless, giving grace and mercy to all who ask.

As this book of wisdom reveals, God presents Himself to each individual according to his or her spiritual need. To all people everywhere, God is the Creator (3:19–20; 14:31; 16:11; 17:5; 20:12; 22:2) and the all-knowing Shepherd of souls (5:21; 15:3; 15:11; 22:12; 24:12). To the stubborn, unrepentant sinner, He is the righteous Judge (8:35; 17:15; 21:3; 22:22–23; 23:10–11; 29:26). To the helpless, God is the Advocate of the weak (14:31; 15:25; 17:5; 22:2, 22–23; 23:10–11; 29:13). To the faithful, the Lord is the Benefactor of the righteous (3:1–10; 8:35; 10:32; 11:1, 20; 12:2, 22; 15:8; 16:20; 18:22; 19:17; 28:25).

For our purposes as readers of this volume, God is the Author of wisdom, whom we cannot—must not—ignore without suffering unwanted consequences in this life and then facing a fearsome reckoning in the life to come.

Reflections

If you received a letter written by God addressed specifically to you, how would you respond? What would you do with it? Because the book of Proverbs offers practical counsel that applies to all people, living in all places, throughout all time, and in all cultures, it can be said that God wrote this book for you! How are you responding to it?

Day 5: *Proverbs 1*
The Purpose of the Proverbs

A s we open the book of Proverbs in order to discover divine wisdom for ourselves, an appropriate question to ask is, why? Why has God preserved these sayings down through the centuries? If we go back to the preamble of the book, we'll find the answer. You might want to glance back over Proverbs 1:1–9. As I reflect on those words, I find five reasons God gave us this book of wisdom:

1. To inspire reverence and obedience within the reader's heart

The opening words of the first section establish the purpose for the entire book in very clear terms: "to know wisdom and instruction" (Proverbs 1:2). Remember, in the Hebrew mind, to "know wisdom" is to put instruction into actual practice. Failing to do what we know to do is the definition of foolishness. Therefore, the chief aim of the book of Proverbs is to bring divine truth into proper focus, enabling us to look at life through God's eyes—from His eternal, all-knowing point of view—and then live accordingly. Proverbs teaches us how to gain wisdom from God's reproofs so that, in the power of the Spirit, we will obey.

2. To teach discernment

"To discern the sayings of understanding" (1:2). *Discern* is a crucial term. The Hebrew term means "to separate; to make distinct." Discernment is the ability to look at a situation and clearly see all its moving parts. A discerning mind has the ability to think critically, to distinguish truth from error, and to anticipate the likely consequences of any given choice.

3. To develop alertness in the walk

"To receive instruction in wise behavior, righteousness, justice and equity" (1:3). The original term translated *receive* carries with it the idea of mobility, taking something along with you, or hauling something. In this case, the student of God's sayings gains "instruction in wise behavior." The proverbs make us alert for the journey of life. Anyone who has driven long distances can affirm that bad things happen—wrong turns at best; fatal crashes at worst—when the driver is no longer alert. These Old Testament proverbs help us remain attentive to our surroundings and aware of potential dangers.

4. To establish discretion and purpose in life

"To give prudence to the naive, to the youth knowledge and discretion" (1:4). The Hebrew concept of wisdom doesn't put ignorance and foolishness in the same category. The term rendered *naive* means, literally, "simple." Those who have not experienced much of life or have not yet benefited from education are like workers without tools or warriors without weapons. Youthful and naive people approach life poorly equipped. Intellectually empty-handed, they cannot accomplish much as laborers, and they remain defenseless against attack. The sages offered this intellectual and spiritual equipment to the simple, to those who are naive and young.

While some readers and hearers will be older than others, none have "arrived" in life's journey. Regardless of age or experience, each person remains young and naive in some respect. The book of Proverbs—and Solomon's section in particular—assures us that these sayings will equip us for life's challenges. To all those who wander aimlessly, lacking purpose and embracing merely a human viewpoint of existence, the wisdom of God offers hope!

5. To cultivate keenness of mind

"To understand a proverb and a figure, the words of the wise and their riddles" (1:6).

These sayings will help us think keenly: divine wisdom will give our minds a razor-sharp edge. Keep in mind such blades require the application of friction if they are to stay sharp. This process of honing causes sparks and is rarely pleasant. Like that hard stone, the proverbs prepare our minds to slice through layers of falsehood to the core of truth in any matter. Divine wisdom gives us the ability to understand more of life's riddles. Before long, the grind of a merely human viewpoint will slowly be replaced by the wisdom of God's perspective.

Reflections

As you review the five reasons God prepared and preserved this body of wisdom, which one most applies to you and your needs? How has a lack of wisdom affected your life? Before we dig into the wisdom of Proverbs, write down on a blank card a few words about how the lack of wisdom has impacted your decisions. Keep the card handy and make it a matter of prayer before you dig deeper in each day.

THE GRIND OF DISOBEDIENCE

Wisdom shouts in the street,
She lifts her voice in the square;
At the head of the noisy streets she cries out;
At the entrance of the gates in the city she utters her sayings:
"How long, O naive ones, will you love being simple-minded?
And scoffers delight themselves in scoffing
And fools hate knowledge?
"Turn to my reproof,
Behold, I will pour out my spirit on you;
I will make my words known to you.
"Because I called and you refused,
I stretched out my hand and no one paid attention;
And you neglected all my counsel
And did not want my reproof;
I will also laugh at your calamity;
I will mock when your dread comes,
When your dread comes like a storm
And your calamity comes like a whirlwind,
When distress and anguish come upon you.
"Then they will call on me, but I will not answer;
They will seek me diligently but they will not find me,
Because they hated knowledge
And did not choose the fear of the LORD.
"They would not accept my counsel,
They spurned all my reproof.
"So they shall eat of the fruit of their own way

And be satiated with their own devices.
"For the waywardness of the naive will kill them,
And the complacency of fools will destroy them.
"But he who listens to me shall live securely
And will be at ease from the dread of evil."

(Proverbs 1:20–33)

Day I: *Proverbs 1*
Reproofs

L et's face it: we are a wayward flock of sheep! It's not so much
that we are ignorant, but rather that we are disobedient. More
often than not, we *know* what we ought to do. Put plainly, we simply do not put what we know into practice. So we spend our days
enduring the irksome and painful consequences of going our own
way. The grind of disobedience is neither easy nor new. Unfortunately, it has characterized the human experience almost as long
as humans have walked the earth. The sayings of Solomon address
this tendency of ours head-on.

According to this ancient teacher, the secret of escaping the
grind of disobedience is wisdom. That is, wisdom in the Hebrew
sense of the term. Biblical wisdom is a process that begins with
gaining knowledge, then choosing to set aside our former ways of
thinking, and then putting this new knowledge into practice. In the
verses you just read (Proverbs 1:20–33), wisdom is personified as
a courageous heroine who stands in the street (symbolic of everyday life) and shouts! She calls for our attention. She doesn't want
us to drift haphazardly through the day; she urges us to engage in

life with purpose, taking her along as our adviser. As I read these verses, I observe three facts related to wisdom:

1. Wisdom is available (vv. 20–21).
2. Wisdom can be ignored or spurned (vv. 24–25).
3. Ignoring wisdom produces grave consequences (vv. 26–28, 31–32).

The deeper we dig into Solomon's sayings, the more clearly we discover what brings wisdom into our lives. The secret? Accepting God's reproofs. Jump ahead for a moment and look at a "completive couplet" with me from Proverbs 3:11–12:

My son, do not reject the discipline of the LORD
Or loathe His reproof,
For whom the LORD loves He reproves,
Even as a father corrects the son in whom he delights.

And while we're at it, look at another even more sobering statement in Proverbs 29:1:

A man who hardens his neck after much reproof
Will suddenly be broken beyond remedy.

Reproof is from a Hebrew term that means "to correct; to convince." I often think of reproofs as God's persistent proddings, those unmistakable nudges, His inner promptings designed to correct our ways. They alert us to the fact that we have veered from His course. They communicate, in effect, "My child, that's wrong! Change direction!" These reproofs—these warnings, proddings, nudges—can only keep us from disobedience if we heed them. We don't want to be like the fool in this modern-day parable:

A man purchased a new car and enjoyed driving it everywhere. Unfortunately, he didn't heed the dealer's instructions to check the oil level at every other fill-up and to have the oil changed every three thousand miles. After a year, he ignored first the smell of burning oil and then the strange, hollow sound of his engine. He had long since covered the annoying yellow warning light with a piece of black electrical tape, so he didn't see the light flash red, and he didn't know why his shiny car rolled to a stop and refused to start. Unfortunately, he had also failed to heed the counsel of his financial adviser, so he couldn't afford a new engine either.

Reflections

What warnings have you sensed but perhaps ignored lately? They can come from the most unlikely of sources—a child, a song, a nagging or sudden sense of foreboding—or from exactly where you'd expect it, such as Scripture, a sermon, a concerned loved one. What has been your response? Is there something you should stop doing? Something you should start?

Day 2: *Proverbs 1*

Danger Signs

Author and pastor Andy Stanley tells of a time when he and a friend drove from Birmingham to Atlanta and, to shave an hour off their trip, decided to use an unfinished section of Interstate 20. Impulsive teenagers, they felt a rush of adrenaline as they eased their car between the words "Road" and "Closed" and then gunned it. They had the entire highway to themselves, so they made great time . . . for a while. Fortunately, they were stopped by a good Samaritan before an unfinished bridge sent them sailing into a swamp.

I must confess, there was a time in my life when I thought I was too smart for warning signs. Let's face it: most warnings are posted to keep stupid people from doing stupid things, like the "Do not eat" warning on packing material. Smart people don't need that kind of counsel. No wonder a young person can conclude that warning signs are for other, less intelligent people. Like Andy, however, I survived my less intelligent moments and lived long enough to discover that warnings are for everyone (especially me!). The decision to heed warning signs not only shows wisdom, but it also reveals both a humble spirit and the willingness to admit that others might have greater knowledge or experience than you do.

Solomon portrayed wisdom as a woman standing in the public square calling for the naive to heed her words of warning. She doesn't plead or panic; she has nothing to lose. She instead cautions that grave consequences lie ahead for those who choose to ignore her. Of course Solomon has the book of Proverbs in mind. This ancient literature contains a large number of timeless reproofs. For example, check out Proverbs 6:23–24:

> For the commandment is a lamp and the teaching is light;
> And reproofs for discipline are the way of life
> To keep you from the evil woman,
> From the smooth tongue of the adulteress.

God's Book stands like a warning sign at the mouth of a deep, dark cave named "Immorality." Many enter; none emerge without injuries. So, in bold, red letters, the Scriptures warn, "Danger! Do not enter!" Through the generations, however, these ancient warnings have been ignored at great cost to people who suffered the dreadful consequences of foolishness.

Reflections

Describe your attitude when you read a proverb from the Bible. Do you take it to heart—as if it were written for you personally—or do you assume it was written for the benefit of others? What does your initial response say about your humility and wisdom?

Day 3: *Proverbs 1*

Out of the Mouths of Babes

Divine reproofs aren't limited to Scripture. While Scripture is God's primary instrument of communication, He will use any means necessary to get our attention when we're headed in the wrong direction. On other occasions, reproofs come verbally from those who care about us, including parents, friends, children, mates, employers, neighbors, a policeman, a teacher, a coach . . . any number of people. Consider these reproofs:

- From children: "Dad, you're sure gone a lot." Or "Mom, you seem pretty impatient."
- From employers: "You're not showing the same enthusiasm you once did." Or "You've been coming in late to work recently."
- From friends: "Is something wrong? Your attitude is so negative!"
- From a wife: "I feel that you're getting pretty selfish, hon."

- From a husband: "You don't seem very happy these days. Are you aware that your tone of voice is harsh?"

Reproofs aren't always verbalized—and sometimes a nonverbal response to our behavior can send a perfectly clear and blunt message like "Knock it off!" The consequences of our behavior can warn, "You reap what you sow!" We might even see our own character qualities reflected in the actions of others.

All of us have certain character qualities that need attention. To ignore them is to choose disobedience, and that choice can lead to devastating consequences. To address our weaknesses is to learn and grow from God's personal reproofs. Pause and review this list of character traits as you recall the verbal and nonverbal warnings of your recent past. Circle the traits that nudge your conscience.

Alertness	Discernment	Love	Sincerity
Appreciation	Discipline	Loyalty	Submissiveness
Compassion	Efficiency	Objectivity	Tactfulness
Confidentiality	Enthusiasm	Patience	Teachability
Consistency	Flexibility	Peacefulness	Thoroughness
Cooperativeness	Gentleness	Punctuality	Thoughtfulness
Courtesy	Honesty	Self-control	Tolerance
Creativity	Humility	Sense of humor	Understanding
Dependability	Initiative	Sensitivity	Unselfishness

Reflections

Examine the character traits you circled as needing attention. For each trait, think of a specific example when your behavior harmed or offended someone. Write an apology to each person and set a time to make things right. Don't put this off! (Another reproof.)

Day 4: *Proverbs 1*
Failure to Yield

Solomon pleaded with his son—and, by extension, with all of us—to heed the warning voice of wisdom. A good question is, why? Why must Solomon plead? Why do we ignore God's reproofs, those in Scripture as well as those that come through other means? Looking back at the sayings preserved for us in Proverbs 1, I discover at least four reasons we do not heed reproof. We'll examine two today and two tomorrow. Prepare yourself. These may sting!

1. Stubbornness

"I called and you refused" (1:24).

See that last word? *Refused.* The Hebrew text uses an intensive form of the verb to convey the idea "directly refuse," "stubbornly refuse," or "emphatically refuse." It is used most often in the Old Testament for defying established authority, for systematically and deliberately rejecting it as in the case of Pharaoh, who refused to let the Hebrews go. In another of Solomon's sayings, the sluggard refuses to get a job (21:25).

In many cases, a strong will can be a positive trait. We praise the Hebrew midwives in Egypt who refused to kill male infants as Pharaoh had ordered (Exodus 1:17). Thank God for the strong wills of Peter and John, who refused to keep silent about the risen Christ after the religious authorities threatened severe punishment (Acts 4:19–20). History records the stories of many courageous men and women who stood alone against popular opinion to defend truth against error. We call these strong-willed, stubborn people "heroes" because they were *right*! They reluctantly defied authority because truth demanded they stand firm. Moreover, they acknowledged and embraced the consequences of their actions, willingly sacrificing their own well-being for the good of others.

Stubborn refusal to heed the warnings of others, however, reveals an arrogant spirit and a dull mind. Pray for humility and wisdom, both of which God longs to provide His people.

2. Insensitivity

"I stretched out my hand and no one paid attention" (1:24).

When Solomon said that "no one paid attention," he used a term that suggests lack of listening or awareness. It would correspond to the New Testament concept of being "dull of hearing." If you have ever tried to penetrate the shell of an insensitive individual, you have experienced God's frustration. You can also affirm the old adage "There are none so deaf as those who will not hear."

Perhaps the best examples of insensitivity and unconsciousness would be pedestrians wearing earbuds. They walk through life in the isolation of their own music studio—literally walking to the beat of their own drum—completely unaware of their surroundings. Try getting the attention of someone lost in iPod oblivion and you understand something of God's frustration.

Though wisdom "stretches out her hand," many people lack awareness and therefore fail to see her gesture and tune out her voice.

Reflections

Which statement is more true of you?

a) *I hear the advice of others, but I generally reject it in favor of what I think is best.*

b) *I often don't hear the advice of others until something really bad has happened.*

Why do you think this is so? Within the next twenty-four hours, have someone you trust offer his or her perspective on how receptive you are to another's advice.

※

Day 5: *Proverbs 1*
Stinkin' Thinkin'

Yesterday, we examined two reasons why people fail to heed the counsel of wisdom—found either in Scripture or other sources—when making choices. Some stubbornly resist wisdom because they are strong-willed and refuse to surrender. Others simply fail to hear wise counsel due to insensitivity. Today, we encounter two additional factors.

3. Indifference
"You neglected all my counsel" (1:25).

The Hebrew term rendered "neglect" has the basic meaning "to let go, let alone, ignore." The idea is that we keep God's counsel from making any difference in our thoughts, words, or actions. An individual says, in effect, "I really could not care less!" Believe it or not, an underdeveloped sense of one's own worth can prompt this kind of response. Psychological studies conducted in the 1990s suggest a strong link between passive-aggressive anger and procrastination. When people fail to accomplish tasks that will benefit them, the problem can be traced back to self-loathing. These studies merely observed and then quantified what Solomon noted nearly three thousand years ago:

He whose ear listens to the life-giving reproof
Will dwell among the wise.
He who neglects discipline despises himself,
But he who listens to reproof acquires understanding.
(15:31–32)

Indifference can also suggest hostility toward God. Like children who fold their arms and intentionally refuse to follow their parents' instructions, we fail to respond to God's counsel. God, however, doesn't suffer the consequences of our indifference. Tragically, we do.

4. Defensiveness

"And [you] did not want my reproof" (1:25).

The Hebrew language is extremely vivid! The original word translated *did not want* means "to be unwilling, unyielding, non-consenting." The image is of one who fights off reproof the way one dodges responsibility when confronted with wrongdoing. The defensive person typically employs one of three strategies:

Denial: the outright refusal to accept the truth of a situation, especially one's personal guilt

Minimization: refusing to see the full significance of an issue or dismissing it as irrelevant

Shifting blame: assigning responsibility to another or justifying one's actions as a reasonable response to the wrongdoing of another

The fool habitually engages in these strategies to avoid pain and suffering, presumably for the sake of self-preservation. Solomon, however, called this a form of self-loathing ("despises himself"

[Proverbs 15:32]). Those are powerful words from a wise man who had seen the lives of many foolish people come to an early, avoidable end because they refused to heed the warnings of the wise.

Reflections

Are you someone who has to learn lessons the hard way, or do you take warnings and cautionary tales to heart? Try to recall the last warning you heard and note it below. How did you respond internally? In the coming week, tally the number of warnings you notice and then appraise your attitude as a way of gauging your response to reproofs.

THE GRIND OF SHALLOWNESS

My son, if you will receive my words
And treasure my commandments within you,
Make your ear attentive to wisdom,
Incline your heart to understanding;
For if you cry for discernment,
Lift your voice for understanding;
If you seek her as silver
And search for her as for hidden treasures;
Then you will discern the fear of the LORD
And discover the knowledge of God.
For the LORD gives wisdom;
From His mouth come knowledge and understanding.
He stores up sound wisdom for the upright;
He is a shield to those who walk in integrity,
Guarding the paths of justice,
And He preserves the way of His godly ones.
Then you will discern righteousness and justice
And equity and every good course.

(Proverbs 2:1–9)

Day 1: *Proverbs 2*
Deep Impact

Our image-conscious, hurry-up culture celebrates people with broad appeal and shallow character. Just look at the proliferation of reality shows featuring people who are famous for being famous. They do nothing, contribute nothing, stand for nothing, and accomplish nothing, yet television and tabloids can't get enough of them. This is nothing new, of course. Every generation raises a bumper crop of superficial image builders. Standing in their midst, however, like oaks among scrub bushes, men and women of strength and dignity rise above their peers. They reject superficiality in favor of depth. They shrug off broad appeal and choose instead to be transparent and authentic. Rather than cut a wide, yet shallow, swath through life, they focus on what they deem important for the sake of deep, lasting impact. They waste no time polishing their image; their interest lies in deepening their character.

Compare, for example, the careers of two American writers—best friends, schoolmates, and neighbors as children—Harper Lee and Truman Capote.

Truman was a lonely, eccentric child with a natural gift for writing. After his parents' divorce at age four, he lived with relatives in Monroeville, Alabama. While other children played, he pursued his obsession with words, grammar, narrative, and stories. The notoriously foppish boy and the tomboyish Harper became fast friends, sharing a great love of writing and literature.

By the age of twelve, Truman returned to New York to live with his mother and stepfather. While in high school, he worked as a copyboy in the art department of the *New Yorker* and continued to hone his craft. Not long after graduation, he completed several award-winning short stories and published his first novel, *Other*

Voices, Other Rooms. While the book spent nine weeks on the *New York Times* bestseller list, it was his controversial portrait on the dust jacket that catapulted him to fame and earned him the public fascination he had always craved. He relished the attention he received from New York society, but he still could not gain access to the rarified company of the "jet set" elite he so envied.

In 1959, he enlisted the help of childhood friend Harper Lee to help him with the research for his "nonfiction novel" *In Cold Blood*. A few years earlier, Harper had moved to New York to become a writer. She supported herself as an airline ticket clerk until friends gave her a priceless gift. On Christmas, she opened a note that read, "You have one year off from your job to write whatever you please. Merry Christmas." They supported her financially throughout 1958, allowing her to complete the first draft of *To Kill a Mockingbird*. Over the next year, she honed and perfected the manuscript, completing it in 1959. As her manuscript went to press, she helped her friend research his book.

In 1960, Harper's novel debuted and became an instant classic, winning virtually every literary honor in existence, including the Pulitzer Prize. More importantly, however, her book became the most influential literary work in the black civil-rights movement since Harriet Beecher Stowe's *Uncle Tom's Cabin*. But rather than seek glory for herself, she retreated from public view and gave her last interview in 1964. When asked about writing another novel, she declared, "I have said what I wanted to say, and I will not say it again."

Capote, on the other hand, rode *In Cold Blood* into the stratosphere of fame. He finally achieved his goal, which was not to create a definitive literary work as much as to become celebrated and enshrined as a great author. In the seventies and early eighties, virtually everyone in America not only knew the name *Truman Capote* but also recognized the flamboyant image of an author who hadn't written anything noteworthy since 1966. Meanwhile, alcohol, drugs, and celebrity consumed the man Norman Mailer once called "the most perfect writer of my generation."[1] In the end, however, Gore Vidal, Capote's lifelong rival, called the author's death "a good career move."[2]

Two uncommonly gifted writers, two completely different approaches to writing. Lee wrote one world-changing story for its own sake and then chose to avoid public praise. Capote wrote for the sake of fame. Interestingly, *To Kill a Mockingbird* is still required reading in most schools.

Reflections

When you exercise your gifts or use your skills, what is your primary motivation? How can you utilize your abilities to become a person of greater depth? How do you think greater depth as a person will affect the impact of your skills on others?

Day 2: *Proverbs 2*
Let's Dig Deeper

This week, let's level our gun barrels at shallowness. Let's allow the sayings we just read to speak out against our times with forceful relevance. I should warn you ahead of time, this may not be easy. Solomon has taken us into a mine shaft, as it were, to a place of hard work, but he will lead us to a valuable discovery.

As I look closely at these nine verses in Proverbs 2, I find that they can be divided rather neatly into three sections:

---

1   Norman Mailer, *Advertisements for Myself* (Boston: Harvard University Press, 1992), 465.
2   Deborah Davis, *Party of the Century: The Fabulous Story of Truman Capote and His Black and White Ball* (Hoboken, NJ: John Wiley & Sons, Inc., 2006), 256.

I. The Conditions: "If . . ." emphasizes the worker (vv. 1–4)

II. The Discovery: "Then . . ." emphasizes the treasure (v. 5)

III. The Promises: "For . . ." emphasizes the benefits (vv. 6–9)

If you're tired of that daily grind of shallowness and you no longer want to "fake it till you make it," good for you! You must remember, however, that breaking out of that mold is awfully hard work. Solomon wrote about that when he presented the conditions of deepening our lives: "If we will do this . . ." and "If we are committed to doing that . . ." Tough talk!

I find four realms of discipline that we must come to terms with if we hope to live beyond the grind of shallowness. We'll examine two today and then two tomorrow.

1. The discipline of the written Word of God

"My son, if you will receive my sayings, and treasure my commandments within you . . ." (v. 1). It is essential that we *receive* God's sayings, that we absorb them on a regular basis and allow them to find lodging in our minds. Few things affect our world more detrimentally than ongoing biblical ignorance. At the same time, we cannot overestimate the positive impact of scriptural knowledge on a society. We need only look to the founding of the United States of America for evidence.

Many scholars question whether the Founding Fathers were professing believers as our evangelical churches today would define the term *Christian*. Regardless, the vast majority at least maintained a Christian worldview, held God in high esteem, revered the Bible as authoritative, knew God's Word well, and adopted its precepts as their moral foundation. All of the above is undeniable. Their knowledge of biblical wisdom led them to first think deeply and then make decisions based on principles rather than pragmatism.

In fact, their scriptural knowledge made capitalism and democracy possible.

2. The discipline of inner desire

"Make your ear attentive to wisdom, incline your heart to understanding" (v. 2). If we read this verse correctly, we must lend an attentive ear to God's reproofs (remember last week's subject?) and cultivate an open heart before Him. The Bible repeatedly warns that we are naturally inclined to selfishness, shortsightedness, and shallow thinking. The English term *fool* appears no less than sixty-two times in the book of Proverbs alone. In no uncertain terms God urges us to remain closely connected to Him:

> The fear of the LORD is the beginning of wisdom,
> And the knowledge of the Holy One is understanding.
> For by me your days will be multiplied,
> And years of life will be added to you. (9:10–11)

Reflections

When establishing plans, making decisions, or solving problems, what practical steps do you follow as you seek divine wisdom? Is this standard operating procedure for you or carried out only in case of emergency?

Day 3: *Proverbs 2*

How to Seek Wisdom

If you genuinely desire God's wisdom, rest assured He has promised not to withhold it. He declares, "I love those who love me;

and those who diligently seek me will find me" (Proverbs 8:17). Here are two additional disciplines that will put you in touch with God's insight, knowledge, and understanding.

3. The discipline of prevailing prayer

"Cry for discernment, lift your voice for understanding" (v. 3).

Perhaps the single most overlooked discipline in the Christian life—and among the most difficult—is consistent prayer. Prevailing prayer. Ongoing, unceasing prayer.

Don't misunderstand. I'm not suggesting we should simply spend more time in prayer. Increasing the number of minutes talking to God should not become our focus. Instead, let us cultivate a mind-set oriented to prayer and a lifestyle that includes a sustained, running conversation with the Lord throughout the day. Plagued by worry? Let that prompt you to unload your concerns before God. Dismayed by conflict? Share them with the Lord and ask for His intervention. Perplexed by a problem? Ask God for insight, understanding, and discernment. Don't save up your problems and questions for a long session later in the day. Converse with God moment by moment as you experience life.

Pray as you go, but don't neglect time for reflection. Be sure to set aside a few minutes throughout the day—five to ten minutes as often as necessary—for solitude, for a place and time that will allow you to clear away distractions and give your mind a break. Nothing mystical or mysterious here, but don't be surprised when clarity displaces confusion.

4. The discipline of daily consistency

"If you seek her as silver, and search for her as for hidden treasures . . ." (v. 4).

We're talking diligence and effort here! The saying calls us to seek God's truths as if we are digging for silver and to search His mind in the same way we would pursue hidden treasures. This is no superficial game! It's an earnest, diligent pursuit of the mind of Christ! While we don't have to earn His favor—and we can be sure that He's not withholding insight to make us work harder—we must nevertheless cultivate a desire for His wisdom that's no less intense than our natural lust for wealth.

Cultivating a desire for divine wisdom begins with the decision to make it a priority and to begin pursuing it. Jesus said, "Where your treasure is, there your heart will be also" (Matthew 6:21). It's a biological principle that you will increasingly value whatever you make it a habit to pursue. Solomon declared, therefore, that our cultivating an earnest hunger for wisdom will be rewarded: "Then you will discern the fear of the LORD and discover the knowledge of God" (Proverbs 2:5).

Reflections

What most often prompts you to pray? For what do you typically ask? There's nothing wrong with asking God to change your circumstances, but prayer also has the potential to change you—your perspectives and values, attitudes and desires. Right now, think of a difficult situation and ask the Lord how He wants you to think or behave differently in response.

Day 4: *Proverbs 2*
The Benefits of Wisdom

Wisdom is its own reward. Even so, Solomon predicted that the person seeking divine wisdom will enjoy significant advantages. Today we will consider the benefits of wisdom *from within*. Tomorrow, the benefits of wisdom *from above*.

1. Benefits of wisdom from within: further wisdom plus knowledge and understanding
For the LORD gives wisdom;
From His mouth come knowledge and understanding. (v. 6)

We have a significant shortage of what Paul the apostle called "sensibility," a trait he considered a trademark quality of spiritual maturity. He urged older men to be "sensible" (Titus 2:2). Shortly thereafter, he encouraged younger women to be "sensible" (v. 5). On the heels of that, he then underscored the same trait in young men (v. 6). And then, yet again, he wrote that all of us who have been born again should "live sensibly, righteously, and godly in the present age" (v. 12).

Imagine how many spiritual problems we could avoid by simply living sensibly, by applying divine wisdom to every decision, whether mundane or life altering.

I recall presiding over the marriage of an older bride and groom a number of years ago. Realizing that both might struggle to adjust to married life, I spent three or four counseling sessions with them before the wedding, emphasizing the importance of maintaining balance and guarding against extremes. I even gave them a couple of projects to work on in hopes of helping them cultivate sensible ways to adjust to each other. Only a few months after their wedding, they were back in my study, glaring at each other. She was furious at him for his refusal to "give her more space."

I suspected that her living alone for so many years might make her more sensitive to sharing her living space and require a lengthy period of adjustment, so I calmly asked what she meant by her need for breathing room. Are you ready? He had taken all the interior doors in their house off their hinges and stacked them in the garage because he "didn't want either of them to have any secrets." He also started checking the odometer in her car when he left for work each morning and again upon returning. He followed up with a verbal interrogation at supper: "Where did you go today? What took you eighteen miles from home?"

That did it! Out of spite, she deliberately spent untold hours in her car driving wherever and then relishing his doubt about her fidelity. Both suffered a serious lack of sensibility. Both needed an infusion of wisdom. Not surpisingly, their marriage lasted a very short time.

That's an extreme example, but you get the point. The internal presence of wisdom, knowledge, and understanding *can* affect how well things go in life and result in great benefits. Not always, but generally speaking, when we operate from a place of wisdom, life runs smoother—and wisdom will *always* help us respond well when things don't go so well.

Reflections

Think of a specific time when wisdom guided your response to a difficult circumstance. How did wisdom help contain the potential fallout of foolishness? What do you think might have happened had you behaved unwisely?

Day 5: *Proverbs 2*
The Supernatural Benefits of Wisdom

Obviously, behaving wisely or sensibly prepares us to respond constructively to difficulties and conflicts. Consider again the examples of Harper Lee and Truman Capote. I don't know if either of them professed belief in Christ. Regardless, we see how the presence or the absence of wisdom led them to experience life very differently. They began in the same small Alabama town, both moved to New York, both achieved phenomenal success as writers, yet they responded very differently to notoriety. The pursuit of fame consumed Capote, who died early and shamefully. Lee affirmed the impact of her novel, but rejected personal glory. As of this writing, she continues to live quietly and, yes, sensibly.

While wisdom helps us shape our own environments, to make them less chaotic and more constructive, God promises even more. He promises not to leave us to fend for ourselves in a corrupt and foolish world. He promises to remain personally involved with us as we pursue wisdom.

2. Benefits of wisdom from above: protection
He stores up sound wisdom for the upright;
He is a shield to those who walk in integrity,
Guarding the paths of justice,
And He preserves the way of His godly ones.
Then you will discern righteousness and justice
And equity and every good course. (Proverbs 2:7–9)

Put simply, living wisely places us under an invisible umbrella of divine protection. By choosing to pursue wisdom, we align ourselves with God against foolishness, dishonesty, misconduct, and injustice. He delights to support us when we become a part of His agenda. Even so, the support He provides doesn't mean we won't suffer. We are, in fact, at war with evil. The world is a battlefield, and like soldiers, we will endure hardships and suffer wounds. Many thousands of martyrs died as a result of the stand they took for the gospel against powerful persecutors. Wisdom brings supernatural, divine protection. His protective umbrella may be invisible, but that does not make us invincible to evil. Not in *this* life.

But God promises that we will suffer less at the hands of evil if we accept rather than reject divine wisdom. Furthermore, the suffering we do experience will be used for our good (Romans 8:28–39). Still more than that, the suffering we endure now is temporary, eventually giving way to a time when those who seek God's wisdom will enjoy eternity, where "He will wipe away every tear from their eyes; and there will no longer be any death; there will no longer be any mourning, or crying, or pain; the first things have passed away" (Revelation 21:4). We receive some protection now and ultimate protection when He redeems the world from its foolishness and evil.

Between now and eternity, wisdom pulls us up from our shallowness, allowing us to both enjoy God's best now and maintain an eternal perspective in the midst of a sinful, foolish world.

Reflections

Think of a time when you acted wisely and found yourself protected from harm. How do you think God was involved in that situation? Sooner or later, you will face a situation in which integrity, honesty, justice, or righteousness could potentially put you in harm's way. How will past experiences of God's protection help you choose wisely?

THE GRIND OF WORRY

My son, do not forget my teaching,
But let your heart keep my commandments;
For length of days and years of life
And peace they will add to you.
Do not let kindness and truth leave you;
Bind them around your neck,
Write them on the tablet of your heart.
So you will find favor and good repute
In the sight of God and man.
Trust in the Lord with all your heart
And do not lean on your own understanding.
In all your ways acknowledge Him,
And He will make your paths straight.

(Proverbs 3:1–6)

Day 1: *Proverbs 3*
The Physics of Tranquility

Worry is one of our more acceptable character faults, right alongside gluttony and perfectionism. After all, everybody worries, and no one quite knows how to stop. Furthermore, the primary victim of worry is the worrier, so it seems harmless enough. But worry is serious business. It not only causes a number of significant physical ailments, but worry can also trigger serious emotional problems, such as depression, anxiety, and even compulsive disorders. More importantly, worry is a spiritual problem, as both a symptom of foolishness and a precursor to sin. Solomon therefore offered a solution to this age-old sickness of the soul.

This passage contributes to a lengthy discourse in which Solomon advised his son on a number of matters. Take note of his many references to "my son" in the first three chapters of Proverbs (1:8, 10, 15; 2:1; 3:1, 11, 21). Solomon devoted a great deal of time and effort to preserving this wise, fatherly advice. In this case, he explained how to find serenity in the midst of chaos and thereby add years to his life and tranquility to his days.

Solomon counseled his son to cultivate good relations with his community, which we might call "horizontal integrity" (vv. 3–4), and to maintain a right relationship with his God, which is "vertical integrity" (vv. 5–6). Both describe a cause-and-effect principle not unlike a law of physics or a principle of life. Drop a weight, and it will fall. Eat sensibly, exercise regularly, and your body will be fit. Live within your means, save money, and you will build wealth. We will examine the issue of horizontal relationships today and then spend the remainder of the week discovering how to maintain vertical integrity.

The sage stated that one can minimize worry by assimilating two key virtues: kindness and truth. The word *kindness* is one of the most theologically important words in the Hebrew culture. The term *chesed* is variously translated "mercy," "loving-kindness," "grace," and "loyalty." It describes the unrelenting, inexplicable, overwhelming grace of God for His covenant people. It is this quality of God's character that causes Him to honor His covenant regardless of Israel's many failures.

The Hebrew term rendered "truth" conveys the idea of firmness or assurance. This isn't about truth as knowledge, but truth as a way of relating: relational integrity. When truth is part of your character, you speak truly, you honor your commitments, and you uphold others who are "true."

When kindness and truth become a natural part of our interactions with others, favor and a good reputation become our reward. These will go a long way toward preventing problems, as well as draining our worry tank.

Reflections

As you reflect on your most troubling problems, which are caused by conflict or poor relationships with others? What worries might you unload by making peace with someone, even if you must accept some pain and loss of some kind in the process?

Day 2: *Proverbs 3*
Straight Talk about Trust

In his fatherly advice about worry, Solomon turned from the horizontal dimension to consider the vertical (vv. 5–6), our relationship with God. There are four verbs in these two verses, four action words that are of special interest to all who want to live beyond the daily grind of worry.

- trust
- lean
- acknowledge
- make straight

The first three terms are commands directed to the child of God. They are our responsibility: "Trust . . . do not lean . . . acknowledge." The fourth verb—*make straight*—is a simple declaration of God's promise, declaring His part of the covenant. The structure of three commands followed by a promise strongly implies another cause-and-effect principle we can rely on. Except this particular cause prompts a *supernatural* effect.

Our Part:

> Trust!
>
> Do not lean!
>
> Acknowledge!

God's Part:

> He will make straight. . . .

Take note also that the possessive pronoun *your* appears four times. This is a personal promise you can trust in at any time. Or not. God leaves that choice to us.

So, the first phrase and the last establish the main idea; the two middle statements merely amplify that idea. The main idea is "I am to trust in my Lord with all my heart—without reservation; in response, He makes my paths straight." The middle two phrases expand on this main idea.

Trust is a dramatically descriptive term. It's similar to an Arabic word that means, literally, "to throw oneself down upon his or her face," a posture that conveys complete dependence and submission. *Trust* refers to mentally and emotionally throwing oneself facedown on the ground—casting all hopes for the present and the future upon another, finding provision and security there. In most Hebrew contexts, the word *trust* carries the idea of feeling safe and secure or feeling unconcerned. To see this more clearly, look at the clever play on words in Proverbs 11:28:

He who trusts in [or "casts himself upon"] his riches will fall,
But the righteous will flourish like the green leaf.

We are told not to trust in riches, for riches are not secure (see Proverbs 23:4–5). If you set your heart on getting rich, if you throw yourself down upon your wealth so as to find provision and security there, you will be sadly disappointed. Riches fail and fly away. What's more, material wealth cannot help you in eternity.

Consider also Proverbs 3:21–23:

My son, let them not vanish from your sight;
Keep sound wisdom and discretion,
So they will be life to your soul
And adornment to your neck.
Then you will walk in your way securely
And your foot will not stumble.

The word translated "securely" has the same Hebrew root word as our term *trust*. We are commanded by our Lord to cast ourselves completely, fully, absolutely on Him—and on Him alone!

The English word *Lord* translates the sacred name for God, expressed by the four consonants YHWH. To this day, Orthodox Jews consider it so sacred they will not even pronounce it. It is the title given Israel's covenant-keeping God, the supreme King of the universe who bound Himself to His people by love and by promise. The New Testament writers—recognizing the deity of God's precious Son—applied the title to Jesus. We are to rely fully upon Him, finding our provision and security in His sovereign care.

The term *heart* has little to do with the blood-pumping organ in your chest. The word is instead used throughout the Old Testament to refer to our inner self, that part of us that constitutes the seat of our intellect, emotion, and will: our conscience and our personality. So what is the Lord saying? He is saying we are to cast ourselves upon our Savior-God in complete trust, not holding back in any area of our mind or will or feeling. That, my friend, is quite an assignment!

Reflections

The command "Trust in the LORD with all your heart" adds a game-changing dynamic to making major life decisions. Think of a significant decision you must make in the near future. As you consider your options and weigh the usual factors, ask and answer this question: which option requires greater trust in God's faithfulness? How does your answer affect your perspective on the matter?

Day 3: *Proverbs 3*
How to Trust God

As we continue our study of Solomon's advice concerning worry, note that the second two lines expand on the main idea to trust in the Lord. "Trusting with all your heart" involves two actions: one negative, the other positive.

Today we examine the negative command: "Do not lean on your own understanding" (v. 5). The term *understanding* is so important that, in the Hebrew text, it appears first in the sentence: "Your understanding, do not lean upon." This word refers to our ability to observe something, gain insight, and discern as a means of formulating a decision. Of course, due diligence is our responsibility. Investigate, seek perspectives, apply logic, and formulate ideas. God doesn't ask us to forego planning or to throw ourselves blindly into decisions. He calls us to give greater priority to trusting Him. Let confidence in God's character, power, plans, and past faithfulness be the foundation of all your decision-making as you exercise sound judgment. (Please read that again.)

Here's a helpful illustration: A young man is convinced God has called him to full-time, vocational ministry. In responding to this call, he recognizes his need for training at a good seminary. He visits the school, considers living arrangements, estimates tuition and cost of living, and even locates a suitable job that will not interfere with his studies. But—on paper—his budget doesn't work. Expenses outweigh income and savings. Even so, he knows God has called him to prepare, so he packs up, moves, and enrolls. Why? Because he places such confidence in God's provision that he won't wait until he has solved all the details before obeying the Father's will.

To "not lean on your own understanding" means that you will not give first priority to your own limited perspective. *Lean* is, of course, figurative, meaning "to depend upon something." One might lean upon a staff, a wall, or another person in order to remain standing. The message is "Feel completely confident in God and do not depend upon your own intelligence, insight, or skill to keep you from falling."

I know a gentleman who suffered a terrible injury while skiing, and he was confined to crutches for many long weeks. Several times I found him panting at the top of a flight of stairs. His hands had become red and sore from his constant use of the crutches. He discovered that leaning on crutches is exhausting.

So is leaning on our own understanding! If you want to spend an exhausting day, try to work out your problems using only your limited viewpoint. Chase down all the possibilities you can think of. When you inevitably hit a dead end, back up and try a new man-made direction. Eventually, you will run out of ideas as well as energy. Then, if you don't trust in God, you will have only one option left: worry.

Reflections

Think of a problem or a dilemma you face now or will likely face in the near future. As you consider the issues involved, jot down all the knowledge or skills you would need to make fully informed decisions and then to act exactly as needed. What percentage of this knowledge or expertise do you currently possess? What will you do to compensate for that lack?

Day 4: *Proverbs 3*

Intimacy with the Almighty

As we discovered yesterday, "trusting in the Lord with all your heart" begins with the decision to "not lean on your own understanding." The second choice calls for us to "acknowledge Him in all our ways."

Acknowledge comes from a simple Hebrew term meaning "to know." This kind of knowledge is personal and experiential. In fact, Hebrew writers used this term as a euphemism for sexual relations between a husband and wife. God's knowledge of His creatures is complete (Genesis 18:18; Deuteronomy 34:10; Isaiah 48:8; Psalms 1:6 and 37:18), and He wants us to know Him just as intimately. Rather than leaning on the human crutches of our own insights or skills, we are exhorted to know God's mind—His character, His values, His attributes, His plan.

The Hebrew word *derek* means "way" or "road." In the figurative sense, it refers to the choices we make and the experiences we encounter as we go through life. God encourages us to know His mind in all those decisions and circumstances. What is more, *derek* can also mean "characteristic manner," as it does in Proverbs 30:18–19:

There are three things which are too wonderful for me,
Four which I do not understand:
The way of an eagle in the sky,
The way of a serpent on a rock,
The way of a ship in the middle of the sea,
The way of a man with a maid.

One visual image associated with *derek* is that of an archer's bow, which has a natural curvature to it. Psalm 7:12 uses the verb form of this root word to picture the Lord as having "bent His bow and made it ready." Knowing God and doing things His way doesn't mean we must sacrifice our uniqueness or conform to a specific manner of living: we don't need to wear these clothes, live like our neighbors, pursue only those hobbies, stay within the lines—far from it! Discover who God made you to be and follow your unique path. Just don't neglect knowing God.

Paul the apostle was, far and away, unlike any man of his time, and there has been no one like him since. He made unusual life choices—remaining single, traveling constantly, devoting himself entirely to ministry—and took a path through life no other could walk. He accomplished more in fifteen years than most people achieve in a lifetime. In addition to evangelizing much of the Roman world, he wrote more than a third of the New Testament. Yet nothing displaced his number-one priority: knowing Christ.

I count all things to be loss in view of the surpassing value of knowing Christ Jesus my Lord, for whom I have suffered the loss of all things, and count them but rubbish so that

I may gain Christ, and may be found in Him, not having a righteousness of my own derived from the Law, but that which is through faith in Christ, the righteousness which comes from God on the basis of faith, that I may know Him and the power of His resurrection and the fellowship of His sufferings, being conformed to His death; in order that I may attain to the resurrection from the dead. (Philippians 3:8–11)

Reflections

We begin to worry when our insights and skill reach their limits. In what area of life do you feel least competent? How can a deeper understanding of God—His character, values, and promises—help you feel confidently "unconcerned" about your problems?

Day 5: *Proverbs 3*

The Straight Way

God has established a paradigm to help us escape the trap of worry. This cause-and-effect principle is as much a part of creation as the law of gravity. He directs three commands to the child of God. They are our responsibility: "Trust . . . do not lean . . . acknowledge. . . ." The fourth verb—*make straight*—is part of a simple declaration of God's promise, His part of the covenant. As we trust Him instead of our own perspectives and opinions, He promises to "make [our] paths straight." This word picture alludes to the ancient practice of highway building. They cleared obstacles, filled in gaps, leveled hills, and cut straight pathways into the sides of mountains. Figuratively, the phrase means "to facilitate progress" or "to turn plans into reality." As we trust God and deepen our personal, experiential knowledge of Him, He will facilitate our progress through life and help us successfully follow the path He has marked out for us (Psalm 139:16).

Now that we have analyzed all the vital parts, let's put the verses back together in an extended paraphrase:

> Throw yourself completely upon the Lord. Cast all your present and future needs on Him who is your intimate Savior-God . . . and find in Him your security and safety. Do this with all your mind and feeling and will. In order to make this possible, you must refuse to support yourself with the crutch of human ingenuity. Instead, study the Lord. Learn about His character, discover His plans for you and the world, be amazed by His love and concern for you in each one of your circumstances. Then He—having been granted full control of your life—will smooth out and make straight your paths, removing obstacles along the way.

Reflections

Think of three problems or situations that prompt you to worry. Formally and preferably in writing, give these matters over to God for Him to handle in His own way and according to His timing. Each morning for the next week, read the paraphrase I have shared. Then, any time those matters come to mind and you begin worrying, take that as your cue to hand the matter back to God and ask for His guidance.

The Grind of an Unguarded Heart

My son, give attention to my words;
Incline your ear to my sayings.
Do not let them depart from your sight;
Keep them in the midst of your heart.
For they are life to those who find them
And health to all their body.
Watch over your heart with all diligence,
For from it flow the springs of life.
Put away from you a deceitful mouth
And put devious speech far from you.
Let your eyes look directly ahead
And let your gaze be fixed straight in front of you.
Watch the path of your feet
And all your ways will be established.
Do not turn to the right nor to the left;
Turn your foot from evil.

(Proverbs 4:20–27)

Day 1: *Proverbs 4*
A Life-or-Death Matter

Make no mistake! Your heart is under siege. Like marauding hordes surrounding a fortress, advertisers, porn moguls, and media mavens scheme to find a point of entry. They lob projectiles and drop subtle baits, looking for weaknesses, and shout taunts, hoping to gain an entrance. They want in so they can bring you under their subjection.

At first glance, you may think I'm being overly dramatic. But take it from a guy whose job involves picking up the pieces of broken lives. I'm offering a glimpse of reality as I experience it and as many others have shared their stories with me. Substance abuse, porn addiction, adultery, abandonment, embezzlement, fraud, double lives suddenly exposed and wreaking havoc on everyone—I've seen the devastation and pain of it all. Interestingly, every case has one factor in common: a heart that gradually became corrupted, beginning with what could be termed a "fatal first." (More on that later.) After we have done a little digging into this subject, I trust you will realize how dangerous this daily grind can be.

As we begin, you may recall that, in Solomon's writings, *heart* rarely refers to the physical organ. We learned earlier that *heart* refers to our inner being, our seat of consciousness, our core of decision-making, the center of our mind, our emotions, and our will. In fact, the Hebrew term appears in this context more than seventy times in Proverbs alone. So when I address an "unguarded heart" this week, I have in mind the responsibility we have to guard our inner selves from enemy invasion.

Clearly, Solomon considered this particular advice a matter of life or death . . . literally. He wrote, "For [these words] are life to those who find them and health to all their body" (Proverbs 4:22). In other words, this counsel will not only keep you from dying, but it will help you truly live. Not merely exist, but *live!* This counsel will also help you enjoy good health and avoid the negative physical consequences of sin.

The core message appears in verses 23–27, which can be outlined this way:

    I. *What* we must do (v. 23a)

    II. *Why* we must do it (v. 23b)

    III. *How* we can do it (vv. 24–27)

Reflections

For the next twenty-four hours, become a careful observer of your part of the world. Take note of how many times something in the media tries to influence your opinion, change your values, or affect your behavior. In fact, keep a tally. Use your imagination and describe the effect on your life if you heeded just 10 percent of these messages.

Day 2: *Proverbs 4*

Your Greatest Treasure

As we examine Solomon's counsel on the importance of guarding one's heart, note that he again directs his words to "my son." Because the Holy Spirit preserved this passage for us, we now benefit from Solomon's wise fatherly advice. Observe his comment about inclining your ear to his sayings and keeping them "in the midst of your heart" (v. 21). Very interesting! For the next few minutes, I want us to direct our full attention to this whole idea of guarding the heart. This is how Solomon put it:

> Watch over your heart with all diligence,
> For from it flow the springs of life. (4:23)

Note three important aspects of this important verse:

1. This is a command: "Watch over!"
2. There is an intensity to this command: "with all diligence."
3. The reason for the command is stated in the last part of the verse—"for. . . . "

Notably, the Hebrew text of this verse begins "with all diligence." As we've seen, Hebrew writers used word order to emphasize an idea, usually placing the most important point first in the sentence. Normal structure places the verb first, followed by the subject, then the object. But Solomon switched this up to stress the importance of his counsel—which, of course, means that God considers the advice crucial. The Hebrew phrase rendered "with all diligence" could also be translated "more than all else" or "above all else."

Solomon created an intricate wordplay with the Hebrew term for "diligence," a term that originally comes from a noun meaning "a place of confinement," a place to be closely observed, protected, preserved, or guarded, such as a walled city. The term alludes to the duty of a gate-keeper or a guard on a watchtower, whose role was invaluable. The lives of everyone in the city depended upon his diligence. Solomon redoubled his emphasis by combining this idea with the command "watch over."

The main Hebrew verb translated "watch over" is *natzar*, meaning "to preserve, keep." This same word occurs in Isaiah 26:3: "The steadfast of mind You will *keep* in perfect peace, because he trusts in You" (emphasis added). The word is used frequently in wisdom literature to describe God as the Shepherd of His people. A shepherd watches over his flocks to keep them from harming themselves, to protect them from predators, and to supply their needs.

In the literal sense, *natzar* describes the duty of a guard in a watchtower. He continuously scans the horizon for approaching armies or nighttime raids. He discerns who may enter the city. And he's authorized to use deadly force to prevent illicit entry. Perhaps a good paraphrase would read, "More than all else to be closely watched and protected (like a city or a bank vault), protect your inner self— your mind, your emotions, your character, your discernment—like a sentry at the gate watches over a city from his watchtower."

Reflections

If you were responsible for protecting secret documents critical to the security of your country, how would you protect that information? Whom would you trust? Where would you keep the documents? Describe your most probable state of mind.

Day 3: *Proverbs 4*

On Guard!

Our study of Solomon's fatherly advice has helped us appreciate the importance of guarding our heart, our inner self. He then explains why. The conjunction *for* could be translated "because." The Hebrew word typically indicates an answer to the question why. We must guard the heart because "from within it" something extremely important occurs.

The Hebrew *motzah* is translated "springs." Literally, it means "the act or place of going out." It is the place from which one comes or to which one goes. The preposition *from* tells us that the context here is a place from which life comes: the inner self is the very source of our lives.

Western Greek philosophy, however, has taught us to think of life as a kind of energy or animating force that keeps someone alive. Some Far Eastern religions think of life in this way as well. In contrast, the Hebrews regard life as the sum total of a person's deeds. They thought in very practical terms, so wisdom isn't determined by what a person *knows*, but by what he or she *does*. To modify a quote from the movie *Forrest Gump*, "Wisdom *is* as wisdom *does*." Similarly, Hebrew writers defined a life as something a person chooses to *do* or *become*. Like a house, a life is built, deed by deed, day by day, resulting in something to be observed and examined by later generations.

According to Solomon's counsel, the inner self is the source of the life we construct as we respond to crises, make decisions, interact with people, and—most importantly—behave wisely. As he stated earlier, "The fear of the LORD is the beginning of knowledge; fools despise wisdom and instruction" (Proverbs 1:7). "In all your ways acknowledge Him, and He will make your paths straight" (3:6). Basically, then, this call to "Watch over your heart with all diligence" is dealing with the will of God—both our discovering it and our walking in it.

Now let's put all the pieces of our research together and see what the verse actually says. A paraphrase based on the Hebrew text might read:

> More than all else to be closely watched and protected (like a city or a bank vault), protect your inner self—your mind, your emotions, your character, your discernment—like a sentry at the gate watches over a city from his watchtower, because this is the source of all the decisions, responses, and deeds that represent your life.

Read that over again, this time very slowly.

When we combine this idea with the truth of Proverbs 3:6—"In all your ways acknowledge Him, and He will make your paths straight"—a more complete picture begins to take shape. Like a sentry on a watchtower, we must keep out anything that would endanger the stronghold of our heart and instead swing the gate wide open for knowledge of God—knowledge of His character, His values, His attributes, and His will. According to Solomon, we have no greater duty than to keep our heart in a perpetual state of readiness, receptivity, purity, and sensitivity.

Reflections

In the early days of computer programming, engineers lived by the motto "Garbage in, garbage out." They recognized that the quality of a computer's output depends upon good data. What kind of input does your brain receive throughout a typical week? What are the sources of these influences? Do those voices affirm or undermine biblical truth?

Day 4: *Proverbs 4*
Good Directions

By now, I trust that Solomon has sufficiently motivated you to guard your heart from invasive, detrimental influences and to cultivate a hunger for knowledge of God. Hopefully, we possess adequate discernment to distinguish between helpful and harmful input. If not, deeper knowledge of God is readily available through His Word. If you are reading these pages, you are most likely reading the Scriptures. (At least, I hope so! This book isn't worth much without the Bible.) So keep up the great work! As you continue reading the Scriptures, you will know the mind of God more deeply and consistently, and your discernment will reflect your intimacy with the Almighty.

Assuming we will possess reasonable discernment, Solomon told us how we can guard the fortress of our inner self. He offered three practical instructions using the word picture of a traveler making his or her way through the world. In summary, he said this:

- Ignore false directions (v. 24).
- Focus on your destination (v. 25).
- Stay on the path (vv. 26–27).

The phrase *put away* is the translation of a verb that means "to turn aside." The object of the verb is "a deceitful mouth," and the adjective rendered "deceitful" carries the idea of something bent or twisted out of its normal shape. Sometimes translated "perverse" or "crooked," this Hebrew word describes truth with a bend in it. Solomon counsels us to avoid people who bend divine truth. He wasn't thinking of mere liars; he had in mind false teachers and diversionary influences. Their messages appear similar to biblical truth. They seem to use common sense. They even seem convincing, but their directions lead to the wrong destination.

The English rendering *put . . . far* stems from the verb "to remove." The adjective *devious* also translates a Hebrew term that means "crooked." *Speech* is literally "lips." The command is to remove from our environment any influence that does not align with Scripture, and we must avoid anyone who distorts the Word of God.

Using the illustration of a road trip, Solomon assumed we will have an accurate map or a perfectly reliable GPS. (I have yet to find a perfectly reliable GPS, but we'll pretend for the sake of this analogy.) He said, in effect, "If someone contradicts your map or suggests you ignore the GPS, get that person out of your car and leave him at the next truck stop. Moreover, ignore unofficial, hand-made signs along the road."

According to this wise, fatherly advice, we must keep our road map handy and refer to it often. That's how we will be able to discern the difference between divine truth and crooked directions.

Reflections

Obviously, the metaphorical road map is God's Word, the sixty-six books of the Bible, and we should heed only advice that aligns with the contents of Scripture. How well do you know the Bible? How often do you interact with Scripture on your own? How many verses have you committed to memory? If you are less than satisfied with your responses, talk to someone at your church about programs that might help you develop a deeper knowledge of God's Word.

Day 5: *Proverbs 4*
Keep It between the Lines

Having convinced us of the importance of guarding our hearts, Solomon urged three specific actions to make this practical. Yesterday, we considered the first: we are to ignore false directions (v. 24). As we said earlier, if someone you have regular contact with habitually gives you information that contradicts your road map or GPS, drop him off at the next truck stop and don't look back! Today, we continue with Solomon's travel motif as we learn how to focus on your destination (v. 25) and stay on the path (vv. 26–27).

Every once in a while it's fun to load up the car and simply go wherever the road leads you, to enjoy the freedom of having no particular destination. Normally, however, whenever you pile the family into the car for a road trip, you have a specific destination in mind and an important reason for going. If you're like me, you plan where you will stop for the night, and you'll have a good idea of where to find food, fuel, and restrooms. In the old days, I marked the route on a current map and highlighted the points of interest to the Swindoll family. Now, of course, a GPS handles all those details.

The point is we believers have a destination: the revealed will of God. And that destination determines the route we must follow through life. Hear Solomon's words of encouragement: "Keep your eyes on the road!" (v. 25) and "Take no detours" (vv. 26–27). You guard the fortress of your heart by knowing your destination and keeping your attention focused on where you're supposed to go. The map has indicated the right course, so as you travel, stay glued to the itinerary. Let me illustrate this with a real-world example.

A young man graduated high school with dreams of becoming a police officer. He attended a college several hours from home, where he enrolled to earn a bachelor of science degree in criminal justice. His freshman year, however, took him on a two-semester detour through parties and mischief. On one occasion, someone dared him to take a license plate from a police cruiser as a decoration for his dorm room. He not only accepted the challenge, but he made it the first of a collection. Over the next several weeks, he acquired a stack of more than twenty police license plates!

Then, the inevitable. A routine room inspection led to his arrest. During his night in jail, he had to face an entire squad of extremely peeved cops. His dreams of becoming a police officer nearly came to an end. Cities don't want to hire officers who have a criminal record. Fortunately, the judge gave the young man an opportunity to have his record expunged in exchange for many hours of community service. He eventually graduated and enjoyed a distinguished career as a police officer. That was grace for a young man who took his eyes off the road. He momentarily forgot his destination, and his foolishness placed his vocational calling in grave jeopardy.

You have a destination. God created you for a specific purpose (Psalm 139:13–16). So He calls you not only to walk uprightly and obediently, but to fulfill your destiny. Therefore it is key to guard your heart by knowing God personally and experientially; by discerning His revealed will; by shutting out all that distracts you from that calling; and by steadfastly walking the path He has ordained. Protect your mind and don't settle for anything less than God's best.

Reflections

What is God's purpose for your life? If your calling is your destination, where are you going? What threatens to push you off the road or head in the wrong direction? What will be your next step in the right direction?

The Grind of Biblical Illiteracy

Then he taught me and said to me,
"Let your heart hold fast my words;
Keep my commandments and live."

(Proverbs 4:4)

My son, observe the commandment of your father
And do not forsake the teaching of your mother;
Bind them continually on your heart;
Tie them around your neck.
When you walk about, they will guide you;
When you sleep, they will watch over you;
And when you awake, they will talk to you.
For the commandment is a lamp and the teaching is light;
And reproofs for discipline are the way of life.

(6:20–23)

Keep my commandments and live,
And my teaching as the apple of your eye.
Bind them on your fingers;
Write them on the tablet of your heart.

(7:2–3)

Incline your ear and hear the words of the wise,
And apply your mind to my knowledge;
For it will be pleasant if you keep them within you,
That they may be ready on your lips.

(22:17–18)

Day 1: *Proverbs 4, 6, 7, 22*

Where to Hide the Bible

Few things are more obvious and alarming in our times than biblical illiteracy. Even though the human mind can absorb an enormous amount of information, mental laziness remains a scandalous and undeniable trend in popular culture and even within the church. Fewer people than ever know the most basic contents of the Bible, and that was not the case until roughly fifty years ago.

The United States is officially a secular nation. From a historical point of view, however, America is very much Christian in culture and character. The Founding Fathers were not all professing Christians, and still fewer affirmed the Bible as inerrant divine revelation, yet virtually all of them knew the Scriptures well, and a Christian worldview shaped their understanding of government. Their knowledge of the Bible reflected their childhood education, which included study of the Scriptures. In the 1960s, however, we began a dramatic shift toward a post-Christian society as atheists, pushing for a truly secular nation, challenging any kind of religious expression observed in the public sector. As a result, America is far more secular and far less knowledgeable about the Bible than we were fifty years ago.

I won't harangue you with a long essay decrying the downfall of spiritual America. I'd rather focus on the good news: there is a solution. While there is no quick-and-easy cure-all that will suddenly eliminate the grind of biblical illiteracy, I do believe that one particular discipline more than any other will ease the burden. When

I began to get serious about spiritual things, it was this discipline that helped me the most. No other decision has been as profoundly helpful to me as memorizing Scripture.

When I was younger, one of the first verses I learned came from the old King James Version, the most common translation at the time. It read, "Thy word have I hid in mine heart, that I might not sin against thee" (Psalm 119:11). A more modern rendering appears in the New International Version: "I have hidden your word in my heart that I might not sin against you." The term *hidden* expresses the idea of treasuring the Bible the same way a miser hoards gold coins, keeping them in a secret vault.

Over the years, I have hoarded Bible verses, gathering a storehouse of them in my mind. I can recall more than one occasion when the memorized Word of God rescued me from sexual temptation. It was as though God pulled down an imaginary shade between the other person and me, and inscribed on the surface were the words "Be not deceived; God is not mocked: for whatsoever a man soweth, that shall he also reap" (Galatians 6:7 KJV). I had committed that verse to memory as a teenager. During times when I felt profound loneliness, Scripture I had memorized rescued me from the pit of depression. Verses like Isaiah 41:10 and 49:15–16, along with Psalm 27:1 and 30:5, have brought me great comfort.

Reflections

When confronted with the inevitable challenges and temptations of life, what resources do you keep ready to help you succeed? Most spiritual crises occur without warning. What do you do to prepare yourself for those sudden and surprising assaults?

Day 2: *Proverbs 4, 6, 7, 22*
Growing Deeper in the Scriptures

Yesterday I stressed the value of memorizing God's Word and talked about how doing so has benefited me in practical ways throughout the years. Memorization, however, is only one of many ways to interact with Scripture.

First, we can *hear* Scripture. This is the simplest, least difficult method of learning the precepts and principles of the Bible. There are plenty of trustworthy Bible teachers and preachers around the world. There are churches and schools, trustworthy radio and TV programs, audio and video recordings, and countless online resources that specialize in scriptural instruction. Except for those individuals whose physical hearing is impaired, no one in the world has any excuse for not hearing God's Word.

Second, we can *read* Scripture. Hearing can too easily be a primarily passive encounter with the Bible, but reading requires more personal involvement—a greater investment of energy—than simply listening to instruction on the Scriptures. People who start getting serious about their spiritual maturity will purchase a copy of the Bible and begin reading. Numerous versions, paraphrases, and styles can be found on the shelves of almost any bookstore, and the Internet offers free access to virtually any translation available in print. To get the most out of reading, you might consider a "through-the-year" Bible: its reading plan guides an individual through all sixty-six books of Scripture in 365 days.

Third, we can *study* Scripture. While I prefer reading a print Bible, many people have discovered the power and convenience of electronic Bible resources. This kind of Bible study makes sense, considering that almost everything else we do involves a computer. Some of the better programs take Bible reading to a completely different level, integrating the Scripture text with links to dictionaries, maps, encyclopedias, photographs, diagrams, and commentaries. A click of a mouse on an unfamiliar word brings a wealth of information to the screen, and you can easily lose the better part of an entire afternoon discovering the background and meaning of just one verse. Combine that kind of study with an online course or one of the many excellent programs offered in churches, and the average believer can be prepared to meet any spiritual challenge.

Fourth, we can *memorize* Scripture. As I stated yesterday, committing Bible verses to memory is the best way to displace alien, unholy, and demoralizing thoughts! In all honesty, I know of no more effective way to cultivate a biblical mind-set and to accelerate spiritual growth than this discipline.

Fifth, we can *meditate* on Scripture. As we hear, read, and study God's Word, our mind becomes a reservoir of biblical truth. We can then think through, ponder, personalize, and apply to our lives these truths we've hidden in our hearts. In times of quiet meditation, we allow the Word to seep into our cells, to speak to us, reprove us, warn us, comfort us, and transform us. Remember these two great verses from the book of Hebrews?

For the word of God is living and active and sharper than any two-edged sword, and piercing as far as the division of soul and spirit, of both joints and marrow, and able to judge the thoughts and intentions of the heart. And there is no creature hidden from His sight, but all things are open and laid bare to the eyes of Him with whom we have to do. (4:12–13)

Reflections

Consider these activities that foster knowledge of Scripture and estimate the number of minutes you devote to each in a typical week.

Hearing _____

Reading _____

Studying _____

Memorizing _____

Meditating _____

Day 3: *Proverbs 4, 6, 7, 22*

Bound to Memorize

Solomon offered several insights about the value of placing God's Word at the center of our lives. Let's begin with Proverbs 4:4, where the wise king recalled the instruction of his own father, David:

> Then he taught me and said to me,
> "Let your heart hold fast my words;
> Keep my commandments and live."

Take note of the words *hold fast*. In the Hebrew, the word translated "hold fast" means "to grasp, lay hold of, seize, hold firmly." It is the verb *tamak*, the same term found in the Isaiah 41:10 statement of God's promise to His covenant people:

> Do not fear, for I am with you;
> Do not anxiously look about you, for I am your God.
> I will strengthen you, surely I will help you,
> Surely I will uphold you with My righteous right hand.

The word *uphold* is a translation of the same verb, *tamak*. This Hebrew word most often appears in these two contexts: God's people holding fast to biblical wisdom (Proverbs 3:18; 4:4) and God holding fast to His people. Scripture knowledge helps you participate in a reciprocal relationship in which you gain a firm grip of confidence in the Bible and God sustains you through difficulties. As God's Word gets a grip on you, it truly does uphold you!

Consider also this fatherly counsel from Solomon:

My son, observe the commandment of your father
And do not forsake the teaching of your mother;
Bind them continually on your heart;
Tie them around your neck.
When you walk about, they will guide you;
When you sleep, they will watch over you;
And when you awake, they will talk to you.
For the commandment is a lamp and the teaching is light;
And reproofs for discipline are the way of life. (Proverbs 6:20–23)

Go back and locate *bind* and *tie*. The image recalls the instructions God gave Israel upon entering Canaan. After commanding His people to love Him "with all your heart and with all your soul and with all your might" (Deuteronomy 6:4–5), God said this:

These words, which I am commanding you today, shall be on your heart. You shall teach them diligently to your sons and shall talk of them when you sit in your house and when you walk by the way and when you lie down and when you rise up. You shall bind them as a sign on your hand and they shall be as frontals on your forehead. You shall write them on the doorposts of your house and on your gates. (6:6–9)

God's covenant people took these words so seriously that they crafted little leather pouches called phylacteries, placed copies of important scriptures inside, and then literally bound them to their right hands and their foreheads. Faithful Jews do this for important ceremonies to this very day. The Hebrews also attach mezuzahs to their doorposts. These small metal containers also hold important, handwritten Scriptures written on strips of paper.

While there's nothing wrong with these traditions—Cynthia and I have placed a mezuzah on our own front door—the Lord's point is more practical. He wants His Word to permeate every household and to penetrate each heart. He wants our culture and lifestyle to revolve around Scripture. It's great to have family devotions, but it's even better to make the Bible as common in conversation as the weather, sports, daily news, public events, or neighborhood happenings.

Reflections

If you want to make Scripture a more natural part of your household culture, the transformation begins with you, regardless of your position in the family. So don't tell anyone but try this experiment: For the next month, set aside fifteen minutes each day to read between ten and twenty verses of Scripture and then think quietly about them. Keep a record of comments people make about changes they notice in you.

Day 4: *Proverbs 4, 6, 7, 22*
The Tablet of Your Mind

Solomon recognized a tragic truth about humanity: we desperately want to do things our own way, and we hate being told what to do. As the prophet Isaiah wrote, "We all, like sheep, have gone astray, each of us has turned to his own way" (Isaiah 53:6 NIV1984). So Solomon urged his sons to avoid mistakes he had made, encouraging them to heed God's Word and to make obedience a lifelong habit.

> Keep my commandments and live,
> And my teaching as the apple of your eye.
> Bind them on your fingers;
> Write them on the tablet of your heart. (Proverbs 7:2–3)

While I encourage regular Bible reading and studying, I cannot stress enough the value of Scripture memorization. Committing verses of the Bible to memory straps the truths of God to your soul. The word translated "bind" really means "to tie together, to bring something in league with something else." It's often translated "conspire." Our word *correlate* also fits. Scriptures correlate so much better when we store them up. We are better able to come to terms with life when certain Scriptures are in place in our heads.

No verses more clearly encourage Scripture memory than these in Proverbs 7. When we write something, we don't abbreviate or confuse matters. Quite the contrary: we clarify ideas when we write them out. The Lord said, "Write [My commandments and My teachings] on the tablet of your heart." Don't be sloppy or incomplete in your memory work. It is essential that we are exact and thorough when we memorize. Without this attention to detail, our confidence slips away. I often think of being thorough in Scripture memory in the same way we plan a flight. Every number (flight, seat, gate) as well as the time of takeoff is precise and important. Commit the wrong information to memory, and you won't end up where you expected!

> Incline your ear and hear the words of the wise,
> And apply your mind to my knowledge;
> For it will be pleasant if you keep them within you,
> That they may be ready on your lips. (Proverbs 22:17–18)

I love those two verses. They constantly encourage me to stay at this discipline! The idea of having God's Word "ready on [our] lips" should convince us of the importance of maintaining this discipline. I say again, nothing will chase away biblical illiteracy like memorizing Scripture.

Reflections

Think of something you memorized earlier in life and can still recite. What other memories do you associate with this recollection? How has it impacted you through the years? What effect do you think memorized verses of Scripture will have on your thought process?

Day 5: *Proverbs 4, 6, 7, 22*

Memorization Made Real

In years past, before the printing press and the Internet made information so readily available, people memorized—precisely, word for word—anything they considered helpful. With the mass production of books, memorization steadily declined. Today, with the Internet in everyone's pocket, the discipline of memorization has all but died. Even so, the human brain is a marvelous creation, still capable of storing away significant passages of divine truth. So let me conclude this week's discussion with three practical tips that have helped me in my own Scripture memory program.

First, it is better to learn a few verses perfectly than many poorly. Learn the location of the book (its name, the chapter, and the verse) as well as the words exactly as they appear in your Bible. Don't go on to another verse until you can say perfectly the verse you've been working on—without even a glance at the Bible.

Second, review often. There is only one major secret to memory—and that's repetition. The brain is designed to hardwire skills and memories as we regularly practice those skills and recall those memories. Think of a skill you acquired many years ago, such as driving a car. After years of regularly using that skill, you no longer have to think about all that you're doing when you're behind the wheel; driving has become a natural, almost unconscious function of your body. With consistent repetition, the ability to recite a verse will become just as natural.

Third, use the verse you memorize. The purpose of Scripture memorization is practical, not merely academic. Who cares if you can spout off a dozen verses about temptation if you fall victim to it on a regular basis? Use your verses in prayer, in conversations with people, in correspondence, and certainly in your teaching. Use your memorized verses with your children or your spouse. God will bless your life and theirs as they see His Word bringing out the best in you. Isaiah 55:10–11 promises:

For as the rain and the snow come down from heaven,
And do not return there without watering the earth

And making it bear and sprout,

And furnishing seed to the sower and bread to the eater;

So will My word be which goes forth from My mouth;

It will not return to Me empty,

Without accomplishing what I desire,

And without succeeding in the matter for which I sent it.

Reflections

Caught in the grind of biblical illiteracy? Scripture memorization is a good place to begin. Many Scripture memory programs are available, but I highly recommend the Navigators "Topical Memory System," which I completed as a young marine stationed on Okinawa. It was instrumental in changing the course of my life. You can find it online at www.navigators.org or by mail at:

The Navigators

PO Box 6000

Colorado Springs, CO 80934

Trust me, you will never regret the time you invest in hiding God's Word in your heart.

THE GRIND OF A TROUBLED HEART

Deceit is in the heart of those who devise evil,
But counselors of peace have joy.

(Proverbs 12:20)

Anxiety in a man's heart weighs it down,
But a good word makes it glad.

(12:25)

Even in laughter the heart may be in pain,
And the end of joy may be grief.
The backslider in heart will have his fill of his own ways,
But a good man will be satisfied with his.

(14:13–14)

Everyone who is proud in heart is an abomination to the
LORD; Assuredly, he will not be unpunished.

(16:5)

The heart of the wise instructs his mouth
And adds persuasiveness to his lips.
Pleasant words are a honeycomb,
Sweet to the soul and healing to the bones.

(16:23–24)

Before destruction the heart of man is haughty,
But humility goes before honor.

(18:12)

The foolishness of man ruins his way,
And his heart rages against the LORD.

(19:3)

A plan in the heart of a man is like deep water,
But a man of understanding draws it out.

(20:5)

Day 1: *Proverbs 12, 14, 16, 18-20*
Counselors of *Shalom*

A major cause of death in our world is heart trouble. I don't mean heart attacks or heart failure; I mean that nearly everyone endures the daily grind of a troubled heart, which often presents as lingering anxiety and low-grade depression. More and more people are experiencing a relentless inner churning, characterized by discontentment, insecurity, instability, doubt, unrest, and uncertainty. A troubled heart lacks peace and struggles to find assurance. One remedy for a troubled heart is a friend who can offer wise counsel.

Solomon understood the value of community when the trials of life begin to take their emotional toll. When we start feeling sorry for ourselves, ungodly solutions to our problems appear more attractive, and malcontents come out of the woodwork. The sage warned that deceit is in their hearts and they counsel evil as a remedy to life's struggles. He urged us to seek "counselors of peace" instead. The term translated "peace," however, describes much more than mere "freedom from disturbance or disquieting thoughts."

The Hebrew word is *shalom*, which combines the ideas of peace, prosperity, wealth, health, completeness, safety, and—most importantly—rest in the sovereign care of God. It's a "kingdom of God" word. This remains the ultimate hope of Jews, who anticipate a quality of *shalom* available only through the rule of Messiah.

According to Solomon, we must seek out advisers who think and speak in concert with the mind of God. They don't merely offer a pep talk or cheer us with humor. Instead, these people of God offer hope and encourage godly responses to life's struggles. Eventually, if we heed their counsel, joy will displace our anxiety and depression.

Reflections

Who is your go-to person when your troubled heart needs *shalom*? What does this "counselor of peace" say or do to provide a helpful perspective?

Day 2: *Proverbs 12, 14, 16, 18–20*

Deep Waters

Whoever dubbed our era "The Aspirin Age" wasn't far off. We live in a time when huge numbers of the world's population use medications to relieve heartache, much of which is stress related. According to a 2011 article, prescriptions for the treatment of depression increased by 30 percent between 1996 and 2007 *among patients with no psychiatric diagnosis.*[3] But for the multitudes who are seeking inner peace, medicine cannot fully relieve the deep emotional pain of a troubled heart. That takes a friend who tunes

---

3   Johns Hopkins Bloomberg School of Public Health, *Public Health News Center*, accessed March 19, 2012, http://www.jhsph.edu/publichealthnews/press_releases/2011/ mojtabai_antidepressant_prescriptions.html.

in to our troubles, and precious few of us are even aware of other people's struggles.

The importance of being sensitive to the needs of people around us can scarcely be exaggerated. Even though you may not be steeped in Bible knowledge, you should realize that God can use you effectively as a counselor, friend, and interested listener simply because you know the Lord Jesus Christ! Naturally, the deeper your knowledge of His Word, the sharper your discernment and the wiser your counsel will be. Job's counselors, for example, dealt with him miserably and spoke unwisely. (You might take the time to read Job 13:3–4; 16:2; 21:34.)

Solomon, however, praised the value of a wise counselor:

A plan in the heart of a man is like deep water,
But a man of understanding draws it out. (20:5)

The thoughts and motives of a person lie deep within, and *deep* in this sense doesn't mean "profound." Think of a deep well or cistern, where reaching the water requires special effort and lots of energy. Similarly, reaching the thoughts and motives deep within a troubled heart requires special effort and lots of energy, but a wise, discerning, insightful friend can help us pull up our feelings and examine them honestly. As one experienced counselor remarked, "The issue is never the issue." We *think* we understand our own thoughts and motives, but very often we're driven by internal forces we do not fully understand.

At any given time, we might need someone to help us examine our inner self, or we ourselves might be in a position to help someone else do the same. Personally, I believe this is exactly what Paul had in mind when he wrote: "Bear one another's burdens, and thereby fulfill the law of Christ" (Galatians 6:2).

Reflections

Who offers you helpful insight when you become anxious or depressed? What habits or disciplines does this person practice that make him or her wise? How can you become more like this person?

Day 3: *Proverbs 12, 14, 16, 18-20*

Three Hearts

Although the daily grind of a troubled heart is common, we often think we're the only one struggling with discouragement, anxiety, doubt, and disappointment. Not so! It's all around us. As I described earlier, a troubled heart beats within every chest, and the kinds of trouble are numerous. I find no less than six specified in Solomon's writings. We'll discuss three today and three tomorrow.

1. A deceitful heart

Deceit is in the heart of those who devise evil. (12:20)

The term rendered "deceitful" describes someone who misleads another such that he or she acts based on a false idea. This deception can be deliberate or simply the result of one fool guiding another. People who "devise evil" rarely think of themselves as dishonest or corrupt. They use deception—starting with self-deception—to rationalize their evil deeds as good, often using an "end-justifies-the-means" argument.

A communist sympathizer once tried that approach with Romanian writer Panait Istrati. Admitting that Stalin's Russia was, indeed, guilty of oppression and persecution, he said, "One cannot make an omelet without breaking eggs." Panait exclaimed, "All right, I can see the broken eggs. Where's this omelet of yours?"[4]

Beware the tendency to rationalize behavior when times get tough—and always keep people who "devise evil" out of your inner circle.

2. A heavy heart

Anxiety in a man's heart weighs it down,
But a good word makes it glad. (12:25)

The Hebrew verb from which "anxiety" is translated literally means "care, fear, sorrow, heaviness." This describes the inner turmoil of one deeply caring about something he or she can do nothing to change. In Hebrew, the word *heavy* is the same as in English: it denotes extreme seriousness.

Earlier, we discussed how the wise counsel of a "counselor of peace" brings joy. A kind, empathetic word of encouragement also has the power to lift the burden of anxiety from the shoulders of someone in the midst of a serious crisis. Uplifting words may not solve the problem, but the temporary relief helps the discouraged one endure the struggle longer.

3. A sorrowful heart

Even in laughter the heart may be in pain,
And the end of joy may be grief. (14:13)

---

4 Quoted in Victor Serge, *Memoirs of a Revolutionary*, trans. Peter Sedgwick (Iowa City: University of Iowa Press, 2002), 278.

We have a saying in the southern regions of the United States: "Sometimes you have to laugh to keep from cryin'." Sometimes the losses in life bring you down to the basics, and it takes all your strength to make it through the day. Like sunlight peeking through the leaves of a dense forest canopy, laughter offers a brief respite from long days of sorrow. During these times, we need someone to remind us that this too shall pass.

Reflections

Heart troubles can be either chronic or the result of temporary circumstances. Of the three kinds of troubled heart discussed today, with which do you most identify? Why? What would you have wanted from a wise friend during this time?

Day 4: *Proverbs 12, 14, 16, 18-20*
Three More Hearts

Solomon addressed no less than six kinds of troubled heart in his wisdom sayings. We addressed three yesterday:

- The deceitful heart—People pursue wrongdoing and cover their tracks by deceiving themselves and others.
- The heavy heart—Sometimes difficulties consume a person's every thought and sap all his or her emotional strength.
- The sorrowful heart—People in the grip of deep emotional pain, grieving a loss or enduring grim circumstances, need all their strength just to get through the day.

Today, we examine three more troubled hearts.

4. A backsliding heart (carnality)

The backslider in heart will have his fill of his own ways,
But a good man will be satisfied with his. (14:14)

The Hebrew term rendered "backslider" expresses the ideas of "turning away" and "deteriorating." The sage used this expression because he understood that we human beings are either oriented toward God, submitting to His will and His way, or we have turned away from God and are pursuing our own agenda. But backsliders will reap what they sow; they will receive no more than what they can earn without gifts of God's grace, and they will endure the consequences of selfish pursuits.

5. A proud heart

Everyone who is proud in heart is an abomination to the LORD;
Assuredly, he will not be unpunished. (16:5)

Before destruction the heart of man is haughty,
But humility goes before honor. (18:12)

The Hebrew adjective translated "proud" and "haughty" means "high, exalted," usually "pertaining to an exalted view of self that is improper and so a moral failure."[5] God detests a sinner's self-exaltation. It's repulsive to His righteous character. What's more, it's a pathetic sight, like watching a decaying corpse try to win a beauty contest.

5   James Swanson, *Dictionary of Biblical Languages with Semantic Domains: Hebrew (Old Testament)* (Oak Harbor: Logos Research Systems, Inc., 1997), 1469.

Humility, on the other hand, chooses the lowly place rather than seeking honor for self. It is honest with self and gentle with others. When we choose humility, God delights to heap undeserved honors upon us.

6. An angry heart

The foolishness of man ruins his way,
And his heart rages against the LORD. (19:3)

Hebrew has several words for "fool." This particular term is not the worst sort of fool who deliberately and knowingly pursues evil; this fool is a dullard who lacks the good sense to do what is right, suffers the consequences of his wrongdoing, and then wonders why God doesn't solve his problems. This fool "rages" against God. The Hebrew term paints a picture of a powerful, sea-churning storm.

Some people remain perpetually angry and depressed because their own foolishness keeps them in a storm of perpetual trouble.

Reflections

Clearly, these last three kinds of a troubled heart are far from flattering. They are, nevertheless, common to all of us to some degree at one time or another. Which have you struggled most to overcome? What were the circumstances? How did you find a cure?

Day 5: *Proverbs 12, 14, 16, 18-20*
Choosing to Bless

It isn't known how many people walk around with undiagnosed heart problems, but the frequency of sudden deaths from heart attack suggests millions. It's difficult to treat a problem—physical, emotional, or spiritual—that you don't know exists. Perhaps you wonder how you can detect spiritual heart troubles. Proverbs 20:11–12 suggests a reasonable approach:

> It is by his deeds that a lad distinguishes himself
> If his conduct is pure and right.
> The hearing ear and the seeing eye,
> The Lord has made both of them.

As you notice, the Lord has given us hearing ears and seeing eyes. I urge you to use them! Open your eyes! Listen carefully! Watch the person with whom you speak! Stay sensitive! Doing so, of course, implies that you talk very little, especially during the initial contact.

Just as important to coming alongside others who are hurting is your seeking feedback from trusted advisers. Ask them to watch and listen and then offer helpful feedback. Tell them you sincerely want help identifying your own blind spots.

Now consider Proverbs 16:23–24:

> The heart of the wise instructs his mouth
> And adds persuasiveness to his lips.
> Pleasant words are a honeycomb,
> Sweet to the soul and healing to the bones.

God is pleased when we choose to allow Him to control what we say and use our words to encourage and edify the hurting people around us. Consider the promise God gave to Moses in Exodus 4:12: "Now then go, and I, even I, will be with your mouth, and teach you what you are to say." Trust in that promise. Who knows? God may want to use you in the life of someone who can't seem to get beyond the grind of a troubled heart.

Reflections

No matter what the condition of your heart, take time to stop, look, and listen to others.

Stop long enough to pray. Ask God for His wisdom to see beyond the grind . . . to realize you are not alone in your troubles . . . to have a renewed sense of peace.

Look around. Become aware of the circle of friends and acquaintances that is larger than your own personal world. Be sensitive. Discern turmoil in others . . . even in your friends.

Listen. Instead of launching a barrage of verbal missiles, ask questions, seek information, and listen. Patiently and graciously hear others. When our words are few, they become more valuable.

The Grind of an Uncontrolled Tongue (Part 1)

There are six things which the LORD hates,
Yes, seven which are an abomination to Him:
Haughty eyes, a lying tongue,
And hands that shed innocent blood,
A heart that devises wicked plans,
Feet that run rapidly to evil,
A false witness who utters lies,
And one who spreads strife among brothers.

(Proverbs 6:16–19)

The tongue of the wise makes knowledge acceptable,
But the mouth of fools spouts folly.

(15:2)

The lips of the wise spread knowledge,
But the hearts of fools are not so.

(15:7)

Day 1: *Proverbs 6, 15*
The Most Dangerous Part

Solomon had a lot to say about what we say. In fact, *tongue, mouth, lips*, and *words* occur almost 150 times in Proverbs. On average, a reference to speech appears five times in each of the thirty-one chapters. Seems to me any subject mentioned that often calls for extended attention in our examination of the book of Proverbs. So we will devote two weeks to the topic of wise uses of the tongue.

A key statement on the subject appears in Proverbs 15:2:

The tongue of the wise makes knowledge acceptable,
But the mouth of fools spouts folly.

You may recognize this as a contrastive couplet: it mentions "the wise" in contrast to "fools." Interestingly, both types of people reveal themselves to others by how they use their tongues. You and I realize, of course, that the root problem is not the mouth, but the heart—the person deep within us. Jesus taught, "The good man out of the good treasure of his heart brings forth what is good; and the evil man out of the evil treasure brings forth what is evil; for his mouth speaks from that which fills his heart" (Luke 6:45). Just as a bucket draws water from a well, so the tongue dips down and draws up whatever fills the heart. If the source is clean, that is what the tongue communicates. If it is contaminated, again, the tongue will expose it.

Reflections
Last week I suggested we spend more time observing and less time responding. I continue to encourage you to observe and—in light of

today's topic—to make listening your focus. Also, as you observe what others say to you and to one another, make mental notes of what their speech reveals about their hearts.

Day 2: *Proverbs 6, 15*
Speech That Wounds

Take a few moments to review Proverbs 15:2, which we will use as our outline as we discuss the destructive use of the tongue. Next week we will concentrate on constructive uses of speech.

I have never known anyone who has not, at some time, struggled to keep his or her tongue under control. Because we are fallen, sinful, selfish creatures, we naturally use words to serve our own interests—often at the expense of others. And of course all of us have suffered the lacerations of another's verbal barbs. As I read through Solomon's sayings, I find at least five unhealthy ways an uncontrolled tongue reveals a sin-sick heart. If this issue of an uncontrolled tongue is one of your daily grinds, I encourage you to pay extra-close attention.

1. Deceitful flattery
Bread obtained by falsehood is sweet to a man,
But afterward his mouth will be filled with gravel. (20:17)

He who rebukes a man will afterward find more favor
Than he who flatters with the tongue. (28:23)

What is flattery? Nothing more than insincere compliments

spoken with deceitful motives. It is excessive praise verbalized in hopes of gaining favor in the eyes of another. The difference between affirmation and flattery is motive. If we hope to say something to another that will ultimately benefit ourselves, it is flattery. If we speak for the ultimate benefit of the hearer, we either affirm or rebuke, whichever the situation demands.

2. Gossip and slander

A worthless person, a wicked man,
Is the one who walks with a perverse mouth,
Who winks with his eyes, who signals with his feet,
Who points with his fingers;
Who with perversity in his heart continually devises evil,
Who spreads strife. (6:12–14)

He who conceals hatred has lying lips,
And he who spreads slander is a fool. (10:18)

A fool's mouth is his ruin,
And his lips are the snare of his soul.
The words of a whisperer are like dainty morsels,
And they go down into the innermost parts of the body. (18:7–8)

Who hasn't been hurt by the wagging tongue of a gossip? By gossip, I mean any talking that causes people to divide into camps. Usually, this speech reduces someone in the estimation of the hearer. Gossip almost always conveys false or exaggerated information maliciously. Throughout Scripture, God reserves some of His harshest rebukes for gossips. He despises this sin.

When you receive information that could defame or harm another, consider these questions and responses:

Does this information involve you or affect you directly?
    If not, let the chain of gossip end with you. If so, discuss the matter only with the people directly involved.
What is the motive of the person who conveyed this information?
    If it is not love, either rebuke that individual or remove yourself from the conversation. If the motive is misguided love, offer to facilitate a constructive conversation between the gossip and the victim.

Reflections

As you continue to focus on listening to the people around you, take note of any speech that qualifies as gossip. Examine your initial response and why you responded this way.

Day 3: *Proverbs 6, 15*
Poisonous Words

Yesterday we examined two kinds of destructive speech that attempt to achieve ulterior motives. When we flatter someone, we deceive that person in order to gain an advantage for ourselves. When we gossip, we lower people in the eyes of others. Both involve deception. Today we will consider destructive confrontation. While it is direct and open, unlike the cowardly ways of flattery and gossip, the effect is nonetheless harmful.

3. Arguments, striving, and angry words

Take the time now to read Proverbs 14:16–17; 15:4; 17:14; 18:6; 25:15; 29:11. You will also profit from a careful examination of the following:

Do not associate with a man given to anger;
Or go with a hot-tempered man,
Or you will learn his ways
And find a snare for yourself. (22:24–25)

An angry man stirs up strife,
And a hot-tempered man abounds in transgression. (29:22)

By *arguments* and *striving* I do not mean the expression of differing opinions or even constructive confrontation. Intelligent thinking and unguarded, open conversation must leave room for everyone to express themselves freely and without fear. Naturally, this will lead to the occasional difference of opinion. Arguments and striving, however, have to do with negative attitudes such as stubbornness and rigidity.

The phrase in Proverbs 22:24 rendered "a man given to anger" reads, literally, "Do not befriend an anger-owner" or "Do not befriend a lord of anger." The adjective translated "hot-tempered" suggests a pot of boiling poison. This kind of person responds to virtually every negative experience with venom because he or she remains angry with everyone and everything. Because anger begets anger, strife follows this person like a dark cloud. The sage warned that this kind of anger can be a learned trait. Associate with a habitually angry person and you will soon become like him or her.

That said, we must recognize anger as a natural, healthy response when someone harms or offends us. Nowhere does God condemn anger as a sin in itself. He warns that *unresolved* anger can lead to transgression (29:22) and may give Satan an opportunity to destroy relationships (Ephesians 4:26–27). God therefore urges us to straightforwardly confront our offenders in order to resolve the issue face-to-face and once and for all. If that person apologizes, "you have won your brother" (Matthew 18:15). If, after several attempts to reconcile, the apology does not come, you may have to "overlook a transgression" (Proverbs 19:11; Ephesians 4:32; Colossians 3:13).

Regardless, anger must not be given a place to lodge in one's heart. It will take root and then overtake its host, transforming him or her into "a lord of anger."

Reflections

Is an unresolved dispute keeping you mentally and emotionally at odds with someone? Have you attempted to address this issue face-to-face in a calm, private discussion? If not, you may consider involving a neutral third party who can help facilitate a constructive confrontation. If all your attempts to resolve the matter have failed, you must release it to God and prayerfully submit to His leading.

Day 4: *Proverbs 6, 15*

Self-Promotion

As you continue your attentive listening this week, keep your ears open for another kind of offensive, unproductive speech. It might seem like a minor problem, but I assure you, the Scriptures take this seriously. I'm referring to boasting, to speech or activities that assume a place of superiority over others.

4. Boasting

Like clouds and wind without rain
Is a man who boasts of his gifts falsely. (25:14)
Do you see a man wise in his own eyes?
There is more hope for a fool than for him. (26:12)

Do not boast about tomorrow,
For you do not know what a day may bring forth.
Let another praise you, and not your own mouth;
A stranger, and not your own lips. (27:1–2)

Boasting most often occurs when we speak too highly of ourselves or our own accomplishments, but it's actually possible to boast without speaking a single word. Some luxury automobiles are marketed as status symbols, as are some upscale neighborhoods and certain brands of clothing. God has nothing against people acquiring nice things if the purpose is to enjoy their use. But when someone purchases items to advertise personal success, that person has become guilty of boasting.

Boasting is really a symptom of a deeper problem known as pride, a condition of the heart that craves attention and loves to take center stage. According to Proverbs 6:16–17, the Lord hates pride and considers our self-exaltation a personal affront. In fact, He places "haughty eyes"—that is, a superior attitude—at the head of a list of what He hates, a list that includes lying, murder, rebellion, and slander.

As the proverb warns, "Pride goes before destruction, and a haughty spirit before stumbling" (16:18). Beware of boasting, both your own boasting and the boasting of those around you. Even if you're not headed for a fall yourself, be careful that someone else's pride doesn't bring you down with him.

Reflections

Think of some examples of boasting you have heard recently. Describe your emotional response toward these individuals. Are you guilty of advertising your own skills, abilities, talents, or accomplishments? Why do you do that? What prompts you to promote yourself?

Day 5: *Proverbs 6, 15*
Don't Talk; *Connect!*

An old aphorism states, "'Tis better to remain silent and be thought a fool, than to speak up and remove all doubt." I can personally vouch for this straightforward advice. In fact, it has solid biblical support. The book of Proverbs warns against this overlooked verbal danger: verbosity.

5. Verbosity

The wise of heart will receive commands,
But a babbling fool will be ruined. (10:8)

When there are many words, transgression is unavoidable,
But he who restrains his lips is wise. (10:19)

He who restrains his words has knowledge,
And he who has a cool spirit is a man of understanding.
Even a fool, when he keeps silent, is considered wise;
When he closes his lips, he is considered prudent. (17:27–28)

Verbosity is the habit of talking too much while saying too little. People who are verbose usually feel compelled to comment on anything and everything, either because they fear silence or sincerely believe that meaningless talk is better than none at all. So these people fill blessed silence with inane talk. They interrupt without hesitation. They speak first and think later . . . if at all! And for all their talking, they remain hard of hearing.

A number of years ago I discovered that it's virtually impossible to learn anything while I'm talking. That's undoubtedly true of everyone. So, rather than fill a conversational void with needless chatter, use the time you have with others to listen well in order to understand more about them. Ask open-ended questions until you find a topic that excites them. More often than not, the conversation will take a meaningful turn as they describe their field of interest and explain why they find it exciting. As they let you into their world, you have an opportunity to learn and gain insight into a realm of that person's expertise. When the time has passed, you haven't merely talked; you've connected.

We used this week to consider several poor uses for the tongue. I hope our examination of these five unpleasant examples will encourage you to exercise more control over that powerful muscle in your mouth. Next week we'll focus on some correct, healthy uses of the tongue. Frankly, I'm ready for the positive.

Reflections

When you're with others, does silence make you feel uncomfortable? Describe your thoughts and feelings when this occurs. How would taking an interest in the life of another ease your anxiety? Think of some open-ended questions you might ask someone you don't know well.

THE GRIND OF AN UNCONTROLLED TONGUE (PART 2)

The mouth of the righteous flows with wisdom,
But the perverted tongue will be cut out.
The lips of the righteous bring forth what is acceptable,
But the mouth of the wicked what is perverted.

(Proverbs 10:31–32)

The eyes of the LORD are in every place,
Watching the evil and the good.

(15:3)

A man has joy in an apt answer,
And how delightful is a timely word!

(15:23)

Bright eyes gladden the heart;
Good news puts fat on the bones.
He whose ear listens to the life-giving reproof
Will dwell among the wise.

(15:30–31)

Pleasant words are a honeycomb,
Sweet to the soul and healing to the bones.

(16:24)

A joyful heart is good medicine,
But a broken spirit dries up the bones.

(17:22)

Like apples of gold in settings of silver
Is a word spoken in right circumstances.
Like an earring of gold and an ornament of fine gold
Is a wise reprover to a listening ear.

(25:11–12)

Better is open rebuke
Than love that is concealed.
Faithful are the wounds of a friend,
But deceitful are the kisses of an enemy.

(27:5–6)

Day 1: *Proverbs 10, 15–17, 25, 27*
A Positive Turn

Solomon said so much about the tongue it's impossible to digest all that wisdom in one week. And because this slippery little fellow we call the tongue gives us so much trouble so often, it's fitting that we return to the subject for a second look, this time from a more positive perspective.

Last week we examined several reasons to bridle the tongue. As James 3:2 states, "For we all stumble in many ways. If anyone does not stumble in what he says, he is a perfect man, able to bridle the whole body as well." In other words, a controlled tongue is the hallmark of maturity. In light of that, how few among us can be truly called "mature."

In our study last week, we uncovered no fewer than five wrong ways the tongue can be used:

1. Deceitful flattery
2. Gossip and slander
3. Arguments, strife, and angry words
4. Boasting
5. Verbosity

What a convicting list! As a matter of fact, I know of very few subjects more universally convicting. Learning how to use speech constructively rather than allowing our tongue to wreak havoc in our communities and relationships is an ongoing challenge. Fortunately, the tongue can become a wonderful instrument of grace, peace, love, and kindness. This week, let's focus on these positive uses of speech as we let Solomon's sayings add soothing oil to the daily grind of an uncontrolled tongue.

Reflections

Think of someone you know whose speech usually has a positive impact on others and generally creates a pleasant environment. What does this person typically talk about? How often do you hear negativity, criticisms, or complaints? Make a study of this person, taking special note of the response he or she receives from others.

Wise Words

Solomon considered both the negative and positive uses of the tongue:

The tongue of the wise makes knowledge acceptable,
But the mouth of fools spouts folly. (Proverbs 15:2)

The lips of the wise spread knowledge,
But the hearts of fools are not so. (15:7)

Just as we found five destructive uses of the tongue, so we find five ways "the lips of the wise" can benefit others.

1. Wise counsel and sound advice
The lips of the righteous bring forth what is acceptable. (10:32)

The lips of the wise spread knowledge. (15:7)

Without consultation, plans are frustrated,
But with many counselors they succeed. (15:22)

Prepare plans by consultation,
And make war by wise guidance. (20:18)

It would also be worth your time to read and meditate on Proverbs 25:19, 26, and 28. These three additional sayings point out the consequences of heeding unwise, unsound advice. We have all received both wise and unwise counsel. How can anyone adequately measure the great benefits of wise, insightful counsel? Usually, you're at the end of your rope: you've exhausted every resource, tried every option, attempted every strategy, and then a sound bit of insight from a wise friend changes everything.

Obviously, someone out of fellowship with God can offer only a limited perspective. Some worldly wisdom can be beneficial, but only when it is subjected to the authority of divine truth. We must use great discernment when seeking counsel and be extremely cautious when advice comes from someone who rejects a biblical worldview. You may be surprised to discover that age and life experience don't necessarily translate into wisdom. Job noted, "The abundant in years may not be wise, nor may elders understand justice" (Job 32:9).

Reflections

Think of a time when wise counsel helped you resolve a dilemma or overcome a challenge. How did you come by this information? Do you have access to wise counsel on a regular basis? Do you have experience or insight you can offer others? How do you make yourself available for consultation?

Day 3: Proverbs 10, 15-17, 25, 27
Friendly Wounds

As we continue to examine the five kinds of constructive speech noted in the book of Proverbs, we must accept that not all constructive speech is pleasant. In fact, the most helpful use of the tongue can be quite uncomfortable for everyone involved—the speaker, the hearer, and bystanders. Moreover, pleasant, soothing words given in the wrong context can lead to disaster.

2. Reproof, rebuke, spiritual exhortation

A fool rejects his father's discipline,
But he who regards reproof is sensible. (15:5)

Grievous punishment is for him who forsakes the way;
He who hates reproof will die. (15:10)

He whose ear listens to the life-giving reproof
Will dwell among the wise.
He who neglects discipline despises himself,
But he who listens to reproof acquires understanding.
(15:31–32)

Faithful are the wounds of a friend,
But deceitful are the kisses of an enemy. (27:6)

He who rebukes a man will afterward find more favor
Than he who flatters with the tongue. (28:23)

Reproof. How rare yet how essential! Pause and think of an occasion when someone wisely yet firmly rebuked your behavior, your thinking, or your attitude, and you became a better person as a result? Look again at Proverbs 27:6. I will amplify it, using the Hebrew text as our guide. Literally the verse reads:

Trustworthy are the bruises caused by the wounding of one who loves you; deceitful is the flattery of one who hates you.

This tells us several things:

* The one who does the rebuking should be someone who loves the person he or she rebukes.

- A bruise tends to linger long after the wounding; it is not soon forgotten.
- Friendship should allow freedom to offer constructive criticism.
- Not all compliments are offered with the right motive.

So much of this matter of rebuking has to do with discernment and discretion. There is a right way and a right time (not to mention a right motive) for rebuking a loved one. If your friend's motive is to help you, those "wounds" will make the best use of timing, be done privately, focus on a specific issue, lead to long-term improvement, and include lots of affirmation and encouragement.

Consider what the sage wrote:

Like apples of gold in settings of silver
Is a word spoken in right circumstances.
Like an earring of gold and an ornament of fine gold
Is a wise reprover to a listening ear. (25:11–12)

These healing "wounds" must be sandwiched between words of affirmation and encouragement. In fact, I prefer a ten-to-one ratio of affirmation to criticism. In other words, when dealing with an employee or a ministry volunteer, I try to affirm and encourage as much as possible. Then, when I must reprove or offer constructive criticism, the person knows that the wound comes from a leader who loves and appreciates him or her.

3. Words of encouragement
A man has joy in an apt answer,
And how delightful is a timely word! (15:23)

Bright eyes gladden the heart;
Good news puts fat on the bones. (15:30)

Pleasant words are a honeycomb,
Sweet to the soul and healing to the bones. (16:24)

By "encouragement" I mean sincere expressions of affirmation and gratitude given honestly to another individual—in public whenever appropriate, in private if that is wiser. We so seldom do this, yet it is one of the signs of a mature, godly individual.

Reflections

How many times each week do you encourage those people closest to you? Think back over the past month and estimate.

Spouse or other significant person _____
Your children _____
Friends _____
Coworkers _____
Employees _____

Look for opportunities to build up those around you with genuine words of affirmation, appreciation, admiration, and encouragement.

Day 4: *Proverbs 10, 15-17, 25, 27*

A Tool for Good

We continue today our examination of constructive speech. While the tongue can cause great damage to relationships and even entire communities, wise use of speech can strengthen relationships and unite people behind divine truth. Preachers, teachers, and evangelists possess this sobering potential.

4. Witnessing, teaching, comforting

The mouth of the righteous is a fountain of life. (10:11)

The tongue of the righteous is as choice silver,
The heart of the wicked is worth little.
The lips of the righteous feed many,
But fools die for lack of understanding. (10:20–21)

The fruit of the righteous is a tree of life,
And he who is wise wins souls. (11:30)

The words of a man's mouth are deep waters;
The fountain of wisdom is a bubbling brook. (18:4)

Death and life are in the power of the tongue,
And those who love it will eat its fruit. (18:21)

Deliver those who are being taken away to death,
And those who are staggering to slaughter, Oh hold them
back.
If you say, "See, we did not know this,"
Does He not consider it who weighs the hearts?
And does He not know it who keeps your soul?
And will He not render to man according to his work?
(24:11–12)

Who can accurately measure the benefits gleaned from the
tongue of a godly teacher well versed in the Scriptures? How can we
gauge the depth of comfort received from the words of a close friend
during a period of grief or affliction? And what about those who told
you about Christ? Remember the encouragement you received from

the glorious, good news of the Lord Jesus Christ? Where would we be without caring, thoughtful people using the gift of speech wisely?

Stop and consider this: "Faith comes from hearing" only when words have communicated the right message, the right way, at the right time (Romans 10:17). God gave humanity the responsibility to carry out His evangelistic, redemptive plan for the world, and we have a solemn responsibility to use words—written or spoken—to accomplish His great command.

Preaching, teaching, or evangelism may not be your gift or calling, but the principle holds true: your tongue can serve no better function in life than that to "make disciples of all the nations" faithfully and consistently (Matthew 28:19).

Reflections

Who is the most effective communicator of the gospel you know personally? What did he or she do to become so effective? What can you learn from that person so you can be a better communicator of divine truth?

Day 5: *Proverbs 10, 15-17, 25, 27*

Choose Joy

It's no secret that I love to laugh. Laughter filled my childhood home, and I hope my children remember their early years as cheerful. I am convinced the Lord has a great sense of humor and that He wants His people to laugh loudly and often. So our study about the constructive use of the mouth concludes on that light note.

5. A good sense of humor

A joyful heart makes a cheerful face,

But when the heart is sad, the spirit is broken.

All the days of the afflicted are bad,

But a cheerful heart has a continual feast. (Proverbs 15:13, 15)

By a sense of humor, please understand that I am not referring to inane, foolish talk or distasteful, ill-timed jesting. By humor, I mean carefully chosen, well-timed expressions of wit and amusing, fun-loving statements. I am convinced of the value of wholesome humor. In fact, I believe that a person without a sense of humor will not be as capable a leader or as effective a communicator as he or she could be.

There are special times when a sense of humor is needed, such as in lengthy, tense, and heated meetings, or when a serious atmosphere has settled in the home, or even after extremely difficult experiences. How quickly and how easily we forget to laugh! Yet medical studies have proven the health benefits of laughter. Look at the last phrase of the final passage I quoted above. The Hebrew text literally says that the cheerful heart "causes good healing."

How do you measure up, my friend? Honestly now, have you become so serious you can no longer enjoy yourself or others? Let's face it, if there is one, general criticism we Christians must accept without argument, it is that we have become altogether too serious about everything in life. We exclude or ignore almost every opportunity for a good, healthy laugh! We're uptight, far too intense, and much too critical of ourselves and others. As a result, our tolerance and understanding are extremely limited. May God loosen us up! And may He ultimately enable us to live beyond the grind of an uncontrolled tongue.

Reflections

When is the last time you scheduled time to have some fun? That's your final assignment this week. Find something that you can share with other important people in your life, something that has fun and/or laughter as the central purpose. Then, enjoy!

THE GRIND OF DISCONTENTMENT

Better is a dish of vegetables where love is
Than a fattened ox served with hatred.

(Proverbs 15:17)

Better is a little with righteousness
Than great income with injustice.

(16:8)

Better is a dry morsel and quietness with it
Than a house full of feasting with strife.

(17:1)

Day 1: *Proverbs 15-17*
Find the Good Stuff

Far too many folks suffer from that most contagious of all diseases. I call it the "If Only" Syndrome. The germs of discontent can infect a single host and then overtake an entire community, affecting every aspect of life—physical, mental, emotional, and spiritual. The following is a list of some statements said by those caught in the "If Only" Syndrome:

If only I had more money . . .
If only I could make better grades . . .
If only we owned a nicer home . . .
If only we hadn't made that bad investment . . .
If only I hadn't come from such a bad background . . .
If only she had stayed married to me . . .
If only our pastor were a stronger preacher . . .
If only my child were able to walk . . .
If only we could have children . . .
If only we didn't have children . . .
If only the business had succeeded . . .
If only my husband hadn't died so young . . .
If only I'd said no to drugs . . .
If only they had given me a break . . .
If only I hadn't had that accident . . .
If only we could get back on our feet financially . . .
If only he would ask me out . . .
If only people would accept me as I am . . .
If only my folks hadn't divorced . . .
If only I had more friends . . .

The list could stretch for pages. Woven into the fabric of all those wistful complaints is a sigh rooted in the daily grind of discontentment. Taken far enough, the "If Only" Syndrome results in self-pity, one of the most distasteful and repulsive of all attitudes. Discontentment is one of those daily grinds that forces others to listen to our woes—but not for long! Discontented souls soon become lonely, isolated souls.

As a wise man once said, "You usually find what you go looking for." So, the question of the day is, what are you looking for? Reasons to celebrate the goodness of God, or reasons to cry, "Woe is me!"

Reflections

You don't have to look hard to find something wrong with everything. But how often do you choose to look for things wholesome and good in your daily experiences? For the next several days, ask yourself this question often: how can God use this for good? Then watch for an answer as daily events unfold.

Day 2: *Proverbs 15-17*

Would You Like Hatred with That?

I am so pleased that Solomon did not overlook discontentment. On three separate occasions he offered wisdom for all of us, especially for those times when we are tempted to feel sorry for ourselves. You may have already noticed that all three of this week's verses are comparative couplets, proverbs in which one thing is declared superior to another. Here is an example:

Better is a dish of vegetables where love is
Than a fattened ox served with hatred. (15:17)

In Texas, where I was born and reared, beef is considered a staple item on the grocery list. In other parts of the United States, a thick T-bone steak is a special treat but fairly common nonetheless. In ancient times, however, meat of any kind was a delight usually reserved for the Sabbath, and then it was typically lamb or goat. Oxen were rarely slaughtered for meat because they were far more valuable alive. When plowing a field, a single ox could accomplish in one day the same work as three men laboring for a week. Consequently, the owner of an ox typically hired out the services of his animal once his own plowing, threshing, or harvesting had been done. It was not uncommon for an entire village to use the same team of oxen for farm labor.

So killing an ox for food in ancient, agrarian societies was a lavish extravagance, not unlike a farmer today selling off a tractor and then using the proceeds to buy the most expensive caviar and serve the finest gourmet cuisine at a single dinner party. Yet the sage who wrote this proverb placed such value on love and harmony that he would rather eat a meager portion of veggies than attend a lavish, sumptuous dinner marred by a hateful attitude and strife. He found contentment in the intangibles of life.

Who needs a T-bone steak? What's the big deal about chateaubriand for two if it must be eaten in the absence of love? Several years ago I smiled when I read about a lady all decked out at a cocktail party trying to look happy. A friend noticed the huge sparkling rock on her finger and gushed, "My! What a gorgeous diamond!"

"Yes," she admitted, "it's a Callahan diamond. It comes with the Callahan curse."

"The Callahan curse?" asked her friend. "What's that?"

"*Mister* Callahan," she said with a frown.

The proverb asks the penetrating question, what good is it to have "more and better" if love and harmony isn't part of the package? The sage gave his answer, stating that the love he shares with his eating companion is always the best part of the meal. It's still truth, isn't it?

Reflections

When sharing a meal with someone, are you easily distracted by imperfections in the food, the service, or the surroundings? How much do love and harmony among the diners affect your ability to enjoy the meal? What can you do to make every meal feel like a four-star dining experience for others?

Day 3: *Proverbs 15-17*

Food for the Soul

As we continue to consider the grind of discontentment, we
have learned that the secret ingredient to a fabulous meal is
love. The book of Proverbs continues this culinary theme with another comparative couplet:

> Better is a dry morsel and quietness with it
> Than a house full of feasting with strife. (17:1)

The image of a "dry crust" (NIV1984) is a word picture any ancient traveler could appreciate. Without the benefit of preservatives
for their food, travelers subsisted on bread or dried meat similar
to beef jerky. They were definitely roughing it. And even at home
during lean economic times, old bread and dried meat might have
sufficed for dinner.

The proverb compares this spartan meal to "a house of sacrifice" (the literal Hebrew meaning). According to Old Testament law
and tradition, a priest was allowed to take home to his family some
portions of meat not completely consumed on the altar (Leviticus
10:12–14). This is how a man who had dedicated his life to ministry supported his household. The term for the ritual killing of an
animal was sometimes used in the sense of preparing for a feast,
for a sumptuous table, covered with delectable meat, vegetables,
bread, and wine.

For the sage, the quality of the meal takes second place to
the emotional environment of the house. He contrasted "quiet"
with "strife." The word *quiet*, however, doesn't refer to silence; it

describes a setting characterized by tranquility, ease, prosperity, and security. The Hebrew term is closely related to *shalom*. So the proverb describes a peaceful, harmonious household where people are free to be themselves without fear of criticism or rejection. There is a sense of ease among the people because strife—disputes, quarrels, and hostility—is not to be found or felt.

The writer of this particular proverb found contentment in most meals because he found far greater satisfaction in harmonious relationships than the most expensive meals money can buy. He might not have been able to control the flow of cash into the family bank account, but he could maintain wholesome relationships under his roof.

Reflections

As you take stock of life today, does your household have a greater abundance of wealth or love? Of material abundance or relational harmony? What are you willing to sacrifice to improve those relationships? If you lack both wealth and harmony, someone has probably given priority to material goods, which *always* leads to discontent.

Day 4: *Proverbs 15-17*

The Thief of Discontentment

By now, the best way to ease the grind of discontentment should be clear. The book of Proverbs counsels us to find personal delight in the things money cannot buy, such as love and interpersonal harmony. Wisdom also points to another intangible hope that satisfies the heart in ways that material possessions fail to do.

Better is a little with righteousness
Than great income with injustice. (16:8)

In the 1980 Boston Marathon, a previously unknown amateur runner named Rosie Ruiz stunned the running world by completing the 26.2-mile race in a remarkable time, just under 2 hours and 32 minutes—then, the fastest woman's time in the race's history. She labored the last several hundred yards looking visibly fatigued, crossed the finish line, and then collapsed into the arms of race officials. The media swarmed around the unexpected winner, who acknowledged training hard on her own to prepare for the historic event.

Unfortunately, Rosie didn't run the entire course. She started, ran a portion of the first few miles, hopped a subway, waited a couple of hours, and then rejoined the race half a mile from the finish. Race officials became suspicious because of her dramatic improvement on her time in the New York Marathon (2 hours, 56 minutes, 33 seconds) just one year earlier. As it turned out, however, she hadn't run that course either. She had taken the bus.

I simply don't understand what one gains from cheating! How can anyone possibly enjoy the spoils of victory knowing he or she could—and probably would—get caught? Rosie Ruiz will always be known among runners as "the marathon cheater."

Nothing obtained by injustice will bring satisfaction. The sage declared that his honest gain, meager though it might be, gave him greater satisfaction than ill-gotten riches ever could. Who cares if your bank account is stuffed and your investment portfolio is the envy of Wall Street, if you cheated to win? That wouldn't make you more successful, more intelligent, more diligent, or more *anything* worthy of respect. Moreover, you must then contend with your conscience. That's like sleeping on a coat hanger: every move you make is another reminder that something is wrong.

The rich and the poor, those who want much, those who have much, and those who feel they need more—all are equally in need of the sage's counsel. Discontentment rarely has anything to do with one's financial status. Greed is cancer of the attitude, caused not by insufficient funds but by misplaced and inappropriate priorities. Some people will never be satisfied, no matter how much they acquire. Discontentment is a thief that continues to rob us of peace and steal our integrity. Ever so subtly it whispers, "More . . . more . . . more . . . more . . ."

Reflections

Name one thing you wish you had in greater abundance. Is it something you can physically touch or purchase with money? Whether your answer is yes or no, consider what you are willing to sacrifice to obtain more. What kind of reaction do you think you would receive if you made this information public?

Day 5: *Proverbs 15-17*

The Choice Is Yours

Let's conclude our consideration of contentment with advice from an older pastor to his younger apprentice. The apostle Paul wrote to Timothy, warning about the dangers of discontentment. The younger pastor served in Ephesus, an ancient city whose economy thrived on the practice of magic and divination, and whose commerce depended upon the influx of pilgrim money to the Temple of Artemis, one of the seven ancient wonders. Money abounded for anyone willing to compromise his or her integrity.

Look at these words of Paul very carefully, as if you are reading them for the first time.

> Godliness actually is a means of great gain when accompanied by contentment. For we have brought nothing into the world, so we cannot take anything out of it either. If we have food and covering, with these we shall be content. But those who want to get rich fall into temptation and a snare and many foolish and harmful desires which plunge men into ruin and destruction. For the love of money is a root of all sorts of evil, and some by longing for it have wandered away from the faith and pierced themselves with many griefs. Instruct those who are rich in this present world not to be conceited or to fix their hope on the uncertainty of riches, but on God, who richly supplies us with all things to enjoy. Instruct them to do good, to be rich in good works, to be generous and ready to share, storing up for themselves the treasure of a good foundation for the future, so that they may take hold of that which is life indeed. (1 Timothy 6:6–10, 17–19)

Note that Paul did not condemn money as evil or even suggest that all rich people should get rid of their wealth. Money isn't the problem, and wealth isn't evil. I've observed that poor people can be more materialistic than a billionaire, and rich people can accomplish great good with their money. The heart holds the key to keeping material possessions in proper perspective. That key is choosing contentment.

Paul cultivated a contented spirit in three specific ways. First, he actively looked for God's working in every circumstance (Philippians 1:12–14). Second, he thanked God for what he had rather than complaining about what he lacked (1:3, 7; 4:11–12). Third, he treasured relationships above material provisions (4:17).

Reflections

Take some time now to put these requests before God in prayer:

- Show me how You can use my present circumstances for good.
- Give me a heart of gratitude for what I have. (Be specific: what are five things for which you are most grateful right now?)
- Help me experience the value of relationships like never before.

Repeat those prayers often as you go through the day and keep your eyes open for specific responses from God as He honors your requests.

THE GRIND OF LUSTFUL TEMPTATION

For the commandment is a lamp and the teaching is light;
And reproofs for discipline are the way of life
To keep you from the evil woman,
From the smooth tongue of the adulteress.
Do not desire her beauty in your heart,
Nor let her capture you with her eyelids.
For on account of a harlot one is reduced to a loaf of bread,
And an adulteress hunts for the precious life.
Can a man take fire in his bosom
And his clothes not be burned?
Or can a man walk on hot coals
And his feet not be scorched?
So is the one who goes in to his neighbor's wife;
Whoever touches her will not go unpunished.

(Proverbs 6:23–29)

The one who commits adultery with a woman is lacking
sense;
He who would destroy himself does it.
Wounds and disgrace he will find,
And his reproach will not be blotted out.

(6:32–33)

Battleground Brain

Solomon was a straight shooter. I find that rather refreshing in our day of vague definitions and bold rationalizations. The words you just read are timeless and no less relevant today than when the ink was still wet. The battle against lustful temptations hasn't declined in the millennia since the wise, fatherly king warned his own children. In fact, we could make the case that temptations are far more numerous today. The opportunity to take a moral tumble arises every time we turn on the television, sit down at a computer, or open a magazine. Make no mistake: we are at war against lust, and we battle for purity from the moment we open our eyes in the morning until we turn out the light at night. The battleground is our mind, and the stakes could not be higher.

Let me remind you that these words and warnings appear in another of the "my son" sections. As a father, Solomon wanted to leave trustworthy counsel and strong warnings for his son to read and to heed. Perhaps the wise king wrote these words with an extra amount of passion since his own father, David, had suffered the consequences of yielding to lustful temptations many years earlier. Although David's adultery happened before Solomon's birth, no one can doubt that he was aware of the consequences that came in the wake of the king's compromising. Solomon was reared in a context that never let him forget his father's moral failure. Moreover, in his adult years, with hundreds of wives and numerous concubines, Solomon had lessons to share from his own moral lapses.

Solomon began with the standard of Holy Scripture:

For the commandment is a lamp and the teaching is light;
And reproofs for discipline are the way of life. (6:23)

God's perfect and Holy Word is always the place to find one's standard of behavior. Not the media. Not other people's opinions. Not books written by fellow strugglers. Not even our own conscience, which can be seared, calloused, or prejudiced. The "lamp" of God's precepts, the "light" of His teaching—these are the things that provide us with unfailing direction. Furthermore, Scripture is the very best antidote to the poison of lustful temptations. I tell you that based on personal experience.

Reflections

Think through a typical day. Name some specific sources of sexual content you encounter, anything that encourages you to linger over sexual thoughts. Estimate the number of times you encounter this kind of stimulus. What effect do you think this has on your mind over time? What can you do to counteract this negative impact?

Day 2: *Proverbs 6*
Flee Temptation

While virtually every outlet in popular media bombards us with sexually oriented material—a phenomenon that previous generations didn't experience—we also face another danger: the opportunities to commit adultery have never been more prevalent. Furthermore, we live in a society that is more accommodating than ever. In addition to the normal temptations that occur in everyday life, we can go online to a dating service for married people seeking affairs!

So what can we learn from Solomon's sayings when we're faced with the lure of a lustful lifestyle? How do we live beyond the grind of this kind of temptation? The sage offered four specific decisions to make to avoid taking the moral tumble of adultery. (We will discuss two of Solomon's points today and the remaining two tomorrow.) He originally wrote these for his son, so temptation is cast as a female. Of course, temptation doesn't discriminate; it afflicts both genders equally.

1. Stay away from the "evil" person.

Solomon urged his son to fill his mind with God's Word as a means of putting distance between himself and the sensual woman he finds tempting. You might not be easily able to escape the physical presence of someone who wants to engage in an affair, but I highly recommend you make any sacrifice necessary to do so. At the very least, you can create emotional distance by nourishing your soul and, if you are married, by cultivating a deeper intimacy with your partner. Bottom line: put space between yourself and lustful temptation.

2. Guard against the "smooth tongue" that invites you in.

Believe it or not, most affairs aren't all about sex. The potential for sexual tension exists anytime a man and woman must spend significant time together, but most people do not cheat on their partners. A good marriage coupled with a secure, God-based self-image keeps us out of trouble. Yet very often, a normally straightlaced person is lured into an illicit relationship with compliments. In fact, sexual predators—aka Solomon's "evil" people—use a person's lack of confidence and relational dissatisfaction as opportunities to conquer.

Observe this vivid scene as Solomon describes how a tempter uses flattery to lure his or her prey:

"I have come out to meet you,
To seek your presence earnestly, and I have found you.
I have spread my couch with coverings,
With colored linens of Egypt.
I have sprinkled my bed
With myrrh, aloes and cinnamon.
Come, let us drink our fill of love until morning;
Let us delight ourselves with caresses.
For my husband is not at home,
He has gone on a long journey;
He has taken a bag of money with him,
At the full moon he will come home."
With her many persuasions she entices him;
With her flattering lips she seduces him. (7:15–21)

Reflections

As you think about your own weaknesses and life circumstances, name some situations or locations you would be wise to avoid. Usually. putting distance between you and potential sin requires planning. For example, one might call a hotel in advance to request a block on adult channels. What will your plan for moral purity include?

Day 3: *Proverbs* 6
Plan for Purity

Solomon warned his son to avoid the wiles of a temptress and gave him four practical instructions to help him. The first two—"Stay away from evil people" and "Guard against the smooth tongue that invites you in"—focus on the external component of temptation. That is, these instructions tell us to place distance between us and the potential lure and fulfillment of sin. This wise father also recognized, however, that part of the problem of temptation lies deep within. Cupcakes appear more attractive to people who are hungry. Therefore, these next two instructions tell us how to survive temptation by looking within and assessing our appetites.

3. Refuse to entertain secret desires for the opposite sex.

Beauty and charm are hard to ignore. Television, movies, advertisements, and virtually every corner of cyberspace train our minds to factor physical beauty into every decision. Attractive people convince us to buy certain products. The political candidate with the more pleasing physical appearance enjoys an advantage at the polls. Impossibly beautiful, air-brushed women stare alluringly from magazine covers, telling us what food we should eat or not eat. Even the newscasters are beautiful! So, why would we expect this preoccupation with physical beauty to stop suddenly and automatically when we interact with regular people at work, home, school, or the marketplace?

Unfortunately, this mental self-control is a matter of discipline. It is neither easy nor automatic. We must consciously retrain our minds to remove physical beauty from our thought processes. We must train ourselves to look beyond it. We must make a conscious, habitual choice to set aside any consideration of beauty and to engage everyone like a brother or sister. We must train ourselves to look beyond it. We must consciously capture all our thoughts (2 Corinthians 10:5) and then evaluate them according to Philippians 4:8 ("whatever is true, whatever is honorable, whatever is right, whatever is pure, whatever is lovely, whatever is of good repute, if there is any excellence and if anything worthy of praise, dwell on these things").

4. Don't let those alluring eyes captivate you.

Everyone wants to feel desired. In fact, this basic need to be wanted has fueled illicit sex since humanity had rules of monogamy to break. Solomon warned that a "smooth tongue" is only one form of flattery tempters use to captivate their unwary prey. A seductive woman also knows how to signal sensual desire with her eyes. In fact, flattery can come in many forms. So beware the charming man who is not your husband or the attentive woman who is not your wife. In almost any context, flattery is merely a prelude to everything you should avoid!

Reflections

When you're feeling unattractive or otherwise down on yourself, to what or whom do you turn for comfort and encouragement? Would the people you respect affirm this choice? Make a mental list of people or situations you should avoid when you're feeling especially vulnerable.

Day 4: *Proverbs 6*

Reasons to Avoid Temptation

We've discussed *what* things to avoid and we've thought about *how* to avoid them, but we haven't explored the question of *why* we should stand strong against temptation. Why did Solomon take such a hard line on resisting lust's appeal? Without the slightest hesitation, the wise man set forth the truth, which so few people stop to consider today.

First, recognize that the sexual tempter goes for "the precious life," the extraordinary person. For some reason tempters fixate on people of great talent, skill, popularity, or potential. When gifted people fall prey to the "evil person," the consequences can be devastating. Everything that once set them apart is suddenly compromised. They risk all these and more:

Loss of character	Injury to career
Loss of self-respect	A ruined reputation
Loss of others' respect	Embarrassment in the community
Loss of family	Draining of one's finances
Loss of Christian testimony	Possibility of disease
Loss of joy and peace	Beginning of a secret life

A second reason to avoid sexual temptation: the pain of chastisement will begin and may never completely subside. Although King David repented, received God's forgiveness and grace, and became Israel's greatest monarch until Jesus, the dark and devastating consequences of his choice never left his home or his heart. In fact, his sons followed in his footsteps, carrying on his legacy of sexual impurity. The one who yields to lustful temptations will indeed suffer . . . and so will his or her offspring.

Third, failure to avoid sexual temptation is clear evidence of someone lacking sense. Solomon likened temptation to "fire" and "hot coals" (Proverbs 6:27–28). Only a fool would try to tuck an open flame into his shirt pocket or stand on the burning embers of a fire. Similarly, only a fool would keep something close by that threatens to end life as he or she knows it.

Reflections

Solomon offered several universal reasons to avoid sexual temptation: these reasons apply to all people. What reasons to avoid sexual temptation are especially relevant to you, based on your temperament, unique challenges, perspective, and position in life?

Day 5: *Proverbs 6*
Lasting Consequences

S olomon concluded this discussion of sexual temptation by considering additional consequences. He noted that when a man steals in order to keep from starving, most people empathize with his situation. Even so, empathy doesn't remove the demand for justice. His community may feel sorry for his desperate choice, but they will neither excuse his sin nor set aside the victim's right to receive complete restitution *multiplied by seven!* Solomon's point: If your community upholds justice in the case of an understandable crime, imagine how severely they will punish the incomprehensible and despicable act of sexual sin with another's spouse! The backlash will be swift and severe. Remember, in those days, the penalty for adultery was death by stoning.

Today, in the age of grace, God has postponed the punishment for sin until the return of His Son at the end of time, when all humanity will stand before Him to be judged. Therefore, if you are "in Christ," the penalty of justice has already been paid by our Savior. The temporal consequences for sin, however, remain, and those consequences may include the wrath of your less forgiving immediate community. Moreover, "wounds and disgrace [the adulterer] will find, and his reproach will not be blotted out" (6:33). A guilty conscience can be dreadful.

Very often, the term rendered "wounds" refers to the sores and resulting scars caused by a disease. "Reproach" stems from a word that refers to the taunts of an enemy or the scorn of honest people after a scandal. These lines describe a ruined reputation and the complete loss of trust among one's community. This ultimate betrayal casts doubt upon the adulterer's credibility in any other context.

Note also another potential consequence: the wrath of the cheated spouse!

> For jealousy enrages a man,
> And he will not spare in the day of vengeance.
> He will not accept any ransom,
> Nor will he be satisfied though you give many gifts. (6:34–35)

Wounds heal, but scars are never completely erased. God's grace abounds, but shame follows the repentant person like a dark shadow. And there are few emotions as powerful, detrimental, or sad as regret ("If only I hadn't . . ."). So don't fall prey to temptation! Don't let your legacy become a list of regrets!

Hopefully, all these potential repercussions make such a strong case against sexual sin that all of us would find it unthinkable. Yet, alas, some will still fall. Many will flirt with temptation, thinking they're strong enough, moral enough, wise enough, or smart enough to avoid actually sinning. But temptation is a slippery slope toward destruction! So resolve today not to focus on avoiding sin; focus on avoiding *temptation* instead.

Reflections

Think of the most worrisome or difficult temptation you face. List the consequences you could suffer if you fall. Some consequences are more likely to occur than others, but list them all. Rank them in order of severity. Keep the list handy for when you face that temptation again.

The Grind of Procrastination

Go to the ant, O sluggard,
Observe her ways and be wise,
Which, having no chief,
Officer or ruler,
Prepares her food in the summer
And gathers her provision in the harvest.
How long will you lie down, O sluggard?
When will you arise from your sleep?
"A little sleep, a little slumber,
A little folding of the hands to rest"—
Your poverty will come in like a vagabond
And your need like an armed man.

(Proverbs 6:6–11)

The soul of the sluggard craves and gets nothing,
But the soul of the diligent is made fat.

(13:4)

Commit your works to the LORD
And your plans will be established.

(16:3)

The mind of man plans his way,
But the LORD directs his steps.

(16:9)

Do not love sleep, or you will become poor;
Open your eyes, and you will be satisfied with food.

(20:13)

The plans of the diligent lead surely to advantage,
But everyone who is hasty comes surely to poverty.

(21:5)

Day I: *Proverbs 6, 13, 16, 20, 21*

Bad Intentions

Pro•cras•ti•nate: To put off intentionally and habitually . . .
to put off the doing of something that should be done. —
Webster's Collegiate Dictionary, 11th Edition

Most of us know the meaning of this word all too well, but a
concise definition helps clarify the issue. The procrastinator usually has logical reasons, valid excuses, and plausible explanations for inaction. Webster's straightforward definition, however,
helps us push excuses aside and focuses us on the core problem:
The procrastinator does not do what should be done. A procrastinator says, "Later," while thinking, "Never." Fulfillment comes
tomorrow, tomorrow, . . . always tomorrow. "Someday, we gotta get
this garage organized" really means, "Everything I choose to do
today is more important than getting the garage in order." People
who procrastinate have no definite plans to accomplish the necessary objective. They simply push it into the slimy ooze of time
indefinite, that murky swamp where every good intention drowns
in excuses.

Let's be honest: procrastination is really self-delusion. The fact is, we have a set of priorities, and we do indeed accomplish whatever we genuinely deem important. In truth, how we spend our time clearly reveals our priorities. We encounter a problem when our deeds reflect a less than honorable set of priorities. So we cover our tracks with excuses and call it "procrastination." Here's what that looks like in real life:

A man *says* his health is a priority. He knows he should devote no less than forty minutes a day to walking, biking, or some form of moderate exercise. Instead, he spends that time on the couch, watching television, eating *baked* potato chips, and sipping *diet* soda. His choices reveal his priorities. In truth, he believes that relaxing in front of the television is a better use of his time than working up a good sweat. Because he can't fully admit to himself his misplaced priorities, he soothes his conscience with the procrastinator's rallying cry: "I'll get serious about this tomorrow."

This, by the way, is a real person's story. He barely survived a widow-maker heart attack. Now he runs no less than twenty-five miles each week! Before his brush with death, he didn't really believe regular exercise is more important than watching television; he only *said* so. The consequences of his procrastination rearranged his priorities. His words and actions no longer live in tension with one another.

Is your daily grind procrastination? Fear not. Solomon's sayings to the rescue!

Reflections

Name something you say is important to you, yet you never quite seem to get to it. How hard is it to admit that you don't, in fact, believe this matter is a priority? Why do you think this is the case? What would have to happen for this matter to rank higher on your "to do" list?

Day 2: *Proverbs 6, 13, 16, 20, 21*
Submit Your Ways

Procrastination can feel like an oppressive ruler who cannot be contradicted or confronted. Its chains appear unbreakable and its rule, absolute. Fortunately, Solomon assured us that we have all we need to break free, as well as an Advocate in the all-powerful, sovereign Ruler of the universe. Hear what Solomon learned:

> The plans of the heart belong to man,
> But the answer of the tongue is from the LORD.
> All the ways of a man are clean in his own sight,
> But the LORD weighs the motives.
> Commit your works to the LORD
> And your plans will be established. (16:1–3)

The ability to plan is definitive of humanity. Orderly thinking is a gift from God and one way we bear His image. Some animals have a rudimentary ability to think and learn ("Sit!"; "Speak!"), but by and large, creatures in the animal kingdom live according to their instincts. They simply do as their animal nature dictates. We human beings, on the other hand, have the remarkable capacity to think things through, to plan our futures, and to alter our environment so we can accomplish those objectives. Horses don't. Rabbits can't. Chickens won't. You and I can, and we should.

According to Proverbs 16:1, we have the ability to set priorities and make plans in line with those, but we cannot make our actions match our words without God's help. That's why Solomon acknowledged that our actions, words, and priorities might not align.

We mollify our agitated consciences with promises to do what we say is important, but God knows our heart motives. In fact, He knows us far better than we know ourselves.

Solomon urged us to stop depending on our own willpower to accomplish important tasks or to fulfill crucial responsibilities. Instead, we must be brutally honest with ourselves and with God as we consider our priorities. He can change our hearts so we will embrace the priorities He wants for us. He can motivate and empower us to do what is right, and He can facilitate our actions so we accomplish His will.

Reflections

Currently, what is the most difficult challenge you face or the most important responsibility you carry? Establish a plan with clearly defined and measurable action steps. Commit this to daily prayer: ask for God's empowerment and submit your plan to His sovereign control.

Day 3: *Proverbs 6, 13, 16, 20, 21*
Examine Your Heart

Two rival foes contend for control of our hearts: Sluggard and Diligence. Locked in a bitter, all-or-nothing struggle for dominance, each uses its most effective weapons to entice us to join sides against the other. Sluggard craves, but he accomplishes nothing. He doesn't follow through. He postpones: "Maybe someday." He tries to convince us that the consequences of inaction are negligible and manageable. He celebrates the advantages of rest and relaxation, and the importance of enjoying life now rather than always sacrificing for the future.

But Diligence?

Poor is he who works with a negligent hand,
But the hand of the diligent makes rich. (10:4)

The soul of the sluggard craves and gets nothing,
But the soul of the diligent is made fat. (13:4)

The acquisition of treasures by a lying tongue
Is a fleeting vapor, the pursuit of death. (21:6)

The biblical evidence is clear, so why don't we always overrule Sluggard and side with Diligence? Why does procrastination appear the more attractive option? I have thought about that a lot. Here are the most credible possible explanations:

We may have set goals that were unwise or unrealistic.
We may have outlined a course of action that appears reasonable, yet we're not completely convinced it's workable. For example, a writer may have a deadline to write a book in six weeks. He outlines how much progress he must make each day. His math is unquestionably correct, and he's not sure he can make it. But a deadline is a deadline, so he dives in, hoping that extra effort will help him accomplish the improbable. Deep in the quiet places of his heart, however, he knows the challenge is not reasonable or realistic. He can't get excited about a doubtful plan.

If you're procrastinating, take a good look at your plan. Perhaps the best course of action would be to adjust your expectations and make the demands more reasonable. Of course, you won't always have this kind of flexibility. When possible, though, commit to a more realistic approach toward accomplishing your long-term objective.

We may have attempted to do something that was not God's will.

We may have chosen to pursue an objective that everyone supports as admirable and noteworthy, yet we lack the assurance that it is part of God's plan for us. For example, a young woman sees a great need for medical missionaries in Africa, so she makes plans to obtain the needed training. She's extremely bright and understands everything in her pre-med courses, yet she struggles with the desire to complete her assignments. She fills her time with extracurricular activities that most would affirm if they didn't take so much time away from her studies.

By the way, this is a true story. It turned out this woman had been called by God to a very different kind of ministry. She's now completing vigorous seminary training to become a Christian counselor, an objective she pursues with diligence and passion.

Your procrastination may be a lack of enthusiasm for an objective you know, deep down, isn't part of God's plan for you.

We may not truly believe our plans are worth pursuing despite the consensus of wisdom to the contrary.

Yesterday I told the true story of a man who put off regular exercise because, in truth, it was not a priority for him. He knew it should have been, but it simply wasn't. Surviving a heart attack that should have killed him changed everything. His near-death experience rearranged his priorities, and he suddenly saw the value of working up a sweat several days each week.

If you truly don't believe an action is worth pursuing, at least have the integrity to say so even if saying it out loud sounds foolish.

Go ahead and let yourself off the hook and admit, "I don't believe _____ is the best use of my time." Then commit yourself to your actual intentions. If it's sitting on the couch eating potato chips and sipping cola, then make a plan and fulfill it. Just remember that choices lead to consequences—and make no excuses when you reap what you sow.

Reflections

We know what we *should* hold as top priorities. But make a list of at least five of your *actual* top priorities even if they sound foolish when said aloud. Then examine how you spend your free time and your discretionary money. This information will point to your actual priorities. Are you willing to make these public?

※

Day 4: *Proverbs 6, 13, 16, 20, 21*

A Big Lesson . . . from a Tiny Critter

Having established that humanity bears the image of God and possesses the ability to make decisions, establish plans, and then alter our environment to accomplish our goals, Solomon turned to nature for a much-needed object lesson. He took us on a field trip to an anthill to discover some truths about motivation and diligence:

> Go to the ant, O sluggard,
> Observe her ways and be wise,
> Which, having no chief,
> Officer or ruler,
> Prepares her food in the summer

And gathers her provision in the harvest.
How long will you lie down, O sluggard?
When will you arise from your sleep?
"A little sleep, a little slumber,
A little folding of the hands to rest." (6:6–10)

Ouch! Solomon instructed us—giants in comparison to these tiny, six-legged creatures—to bend down and to learn from the ant's ways. And what lessons they have to teach! These miniature pedagogues model several valuable principles:

- Ants work for the survival of the colony, a compelling motivation.
- Ants know what to do; they don't need a superintendent prodding them.
- Ants get the essentials done first so they can relax later.
- Ants work without fanfare or applause.

Individual ants know their duty, and their motivation is clear: survival. This keeps them at their tasks despite the lack of short-term rewards. Solomon warned that if we don't become at least as wise as an ant, "poverty will come in like a vagabond, and . . . need like an armed man" (6:11). Procrastinators, however, do not truly believe that any consequences will apply to them.

Reflections

Yesterday you compiled a list of your actual priorities. Today, name at least five priorities you think should top your list. Now, beside each, describe the consequences of neglecting those priorities. Name the people who will experience negative consequences as well. Are these consequences acceptable to you?

Day 5: *Proverbs 6, 13, 16, 20, 21*
Rewards along the Way

Having thought about procrastination, motivation, diligence, and consequences, Solomon and other wise men wrote the following lines of encouragement:

> The hope of the righteous is gladness,
> But the expectation of the wicked perishes. (10:28)

> Hope deferred makes the heart sick,
> But desire fulfilled is a tree of life. (13:12)

> Desire realized is sweet to the soul,
> But it is an abomination to fools to turn away from evil.
> (13:19)

These Hebrew sages acknowledged the difficulty of delaying gratification. They were people just like us, whose hearts get "sick" when forced to put desires on hold. They, too, wanted the immediate payoff of procrastination rather than having to sacrifice to gain the rewards of diligence. They, like us, wearied of working day in and day out to create a good future for themselves. They, like all people, struggled to maintain a balance between enjoying today and planning for tomorrow. Because they recognized the universal desire to take it easy, the wise men of Israel nurtured a robust sense of hope. When you hope, you bring a small piece of future enjoyment into today. When you hope, you imagine the satisfaction you will feel when your diligence begins to pay off.

When I have a big task to accomplish, I plan a vacation that will begin soon after I meet the deadline. That gives me a near-term reward for my diligence. For example, I might plan a week on Kauai to follow several months of intense planning, studying, writing, and editing a major book. (By the way, I don't allow anything I do for the radio ministry or for books to take away from my normal duties as senior pastor at Stonebriar Community Church.) As I diligently complete the manuscript, desperately wanting to quit at times, I imagine myself relaxing on a lanai, feet up, sipping a cool beverage, reading a great book, and enjoying the gentle ocean breeze and the sound of surf.

This works so well, in fact, that I'm inspired to begin another chapter today!

Reflections

What long, difficult, unpleasant task must you complete? List the benefits of completing this assignment on time and with excellence accompanied by a positive attitude. With many duties, the benefits may not be seen for a long time yet. So how can you reward yourself along the way . . . and immediately upon completion?

THE GRIND OF DOMESTIC DISHARMONY

By wisdom a house is built,
And by understanding it is established;
And by knowledge the rooms are filled
With all precious and pleasant riches.

(Proverbs 24:3–4)

Day 1: *Proverbs 24*
Suffering but Not Silent

Of all the grinds that erode our peace, none is more nagging, more draining, more painful than disharmony at home. Sarcastic infighting. Stinging put-downs. Withering stares. Deafening silence. Volatile explosions of anger. Occasionally, emotional brutality and physical abuse. A television blaring in the living room. A stack of dirty dishes sitting in the sink. Doors slammed shut. Desperate feelings of loneliness. Perhaps even dark clouds of fear and dread. Sadly, some of those phrases may describe where you live. If so, you are not alone. In fact, Solomon and other wise men of Israel knew the sorrow and heartache of domestic discord. They wrote from personal experience:

> A foolish son is destruction to his father,
> And the contentions of a wife are a constant dripping. (19:13)

It is better to live in a desert land
Than with a contentious and vexing woman.
There is precious treasure and oil in the dwelling of the wise,
But a foolish man swallows it up. (21:19–20)

The north wind brings forth rain,
And a backbiting tongue, an angry countenance.
It is better to live in a corner of the roof
Than in a house shared with a contentious woman.
(25:23–24)

These writers were men, so they naturally wrote from the husband's perspective. Even so, the principles work both ways, for both men and women who are trying to maintain a peaceful, productive household. As any soul-weary wife can attest, "It is better to live in a corner of the roof than in a house shared with a contentious *man*."

It is possible that you have gotten to the point where you look for excuses to be away from home, or you try to keep yourself occupied in some other part of the house as much as possible. Perhaps you wonder what can be done to restore harmony, to make things different. You may think that change is impossible, but I have good news: it is not. The remedies for domestic disharmony are neither easy nor automatic. But you do not have to merely endure in silence.

Reflections

Describe the emotional atmosphere of your home. Who sets the general tone? How does this tone impact the youngest members of the household and how do they respond? How much influence do you think you have in shaping the emotional environment?

Day 2: *Proverbs 24*

Bedrock

The grind of domestic disharmony can be the most distressing of all. After all, home should be a place of rest and safety, a refuge from the stresses and dangers of the world. For many, however, home is a battlefield where the most intense struggles of the day take place.

As we consider possible remedies for this daily grind, we turn to the wise men of Israel, who described three essential ingredients that turn a house into a home. Hopefully, the patriarch and matriarch, together, establish their union on this foundation, starting from the first day of marriage, and then build their household and family upon them.

Read Proverbs 24:3–4 again. We'll examine one of the three elements on each of the next three days.

1. By wisdom a house is built.

The Hebrew verb *hakam*, "to be wise," and its derivatives are the most commonly used terms denoting intelligence. This kind of wisdom refers to perception with discernment. The original Hebrew word emphasizes accuracy as well as the ability to sense what is beneath the surface. Wisdom refuses to skate across the surface and ignore what is deep within: wisdom penetrates. This kind of wisdom also represents a manner of thinking and attitude that results in prudent, sensible living.

This variety of wisdom, however, goes beyond mere reasonableness and sensibility. As one commentator put it, "The wisdom of the [Old Testament], however, is quite distinct from other ancient world views. . . . Reflected in [Old Testament] wisdom is the teaching of a personal God who is holy and just and who expects those who know him to exhibit his character in the many practical affairs of life."[6] This is a crucial distinction! A household is to be built on obedience to God in every practical human experience of life. A household is to be built upon Dad's and Mom's decision to have their actions fit into the plan of God.

If we want to think of a house as a structure, this variety of wisdom is bedrock. If the husband and wife do not first establish their marriage on a commitment to know God personally and to translate their relationship with Him into practical living, their family and their household will not be stable.

Very early in our marriage, my wife, Cynthia, and I made a commitment to one another. In a very solemn moment in tiny apartment #9 on the campus of Dallas Theological Seminary, we mutually agreed, "Whatever the Bible says, we will do." If ever we have a disagreement, we consult the Scriptures not as a means of coercing one another, but in a spirit of seeking God's mind—as we allow the Word of God to become our tiebreaker.

Our marriage is far from perfect, but we have a reasonably good partnership. Our household with our four children was not without significant problems at times, but this commitment—I am convinced—saved our home from self-destruction and gave our children a stable platform from which to launch their own lives.

Reflections

Ideally, a married couple should make this commitment together, but that isn't always possible. Even so, nothing prevents you from committing to this kind of wisdom as a single head of the household or as one partner in a marriage. Take some time now to lay

---

6   Louis Goldberg, "647 hakam," in Theological Wordbook of the Old Testament, ed. R. Laird Harris, Gleason L. Archer Jr. and Bruce K. Waltke, electronic ed. (Chicago: Moody Press, 1999), 283.

this foundation in your own life. Meditate on this commitment the rest of today.

🕯

Day 3: *Proverbs 24*
Teamwork

Yesterday we looked at the foundation of a stable household: the first layer is wisdom, from the Hebrew *hakam*. This kind of wisdom is the commitment to translate our knowledge of God and His ways into practical living. We dedicate ourselves to making decisions that carry out His plans for our lives, our household, and the world.

Upon this bedrock, the sages erected the structure through understanding.

2. By understanding it is established.

The Hebrew term for "understanding" is *tebuna*, which refers to intelligence or discernment. This word describes our ability to observe, gain insight, and then discern as a means of devising a plan or making a decision. As stated before, we do our homework, investigate, seek multiple perspectives, use common-sense logic, and then formulate ideas.

The Hebrew word rendered "established" carries the idea of forming something over time. The root word means "to be firm," although the context always involves forming or fashioning. Frequently, the idea of preparation is primary. As one lexicon stated, "The root meaning is to bring something into being with the consequence that its existence is a certainty."[7]

---

7   John N. Oswalt, "964 *kun*," in *Theological Wordbook of the Old Testament*, ed. R. Laird Harris, Gleason L. Archer Jr. and Bruce K. Waltke, electronic ed. (Chicago: Moody Press, 1999), 433.

Taking the two terms together, we see both process and progress taking place. Understanding is insight that comes by study. It is progressive: it increases over time as lessons are learned from mistakes and success builds upon past victories. As understanding develops, the house comes into existence. If we continue our building metaphor, understanding erects the walls, puts the roof on top, and installs everything needed to make the house suitable for move-in.

In terms of application, I suggest this describes the practical, professional means of provision and security for the household. The home's existence becomes a certainty as the father and mother do their respective parts to earn a reliable income and to protect the household from loss. This kind of understanding sees to the practical needs of the family. A home is established as each member faithfully does what he or she must do, as each fulfills his or her responsibility.

When one or more members of the family fail to do what must be done, the household struggles. Conflict ensues. Fear and resentment take up residence, causing friction and creating fractures. The very existence of the home becomes threatened.

Reflections

Make a list of each person in your household and describe their assigned responsibilities. Are these duties age appropriate, reasonable, fairly distributed, and clearly understood by all? What keeps everyone accountable? How well does your household function in a practical sense? Are you truly a family or a cast of characters living under the same roof? Explain why.

Day 4: *Proverbs 24*
Rich Relationships

Let's review the building analogy. Wisdom has laid a solid foundation for the home, and the household leaders are committed to making God's Word their standard operating procedure. Upon this bedrock, the domestic structure rises. Thanks to the adults' skillful understanding, the practical needs of the home are met, and the household takes form.

A house, however, is not a home. A home needs people to fill the rooms.

3. By knowledge the rooms are filled with all precious and pleasant riches.

The Hebrew term for *knowledge* is based on the verb *yada*, "to know," and *yada* refers to understanding with insight. One gains this kind of knowledge through intimate personal experience with a matter. The Old Testament uses *yada* to describe God's penetrating knowledge of each person (Genesis 18:19; Deuteronomy 34:10; Isaiah 48:8; Psalms 1:6; 37:18). Scripture also uses this word in reference to sexual intercourse because, in normal, healthy relationships, the couple gains exclusive and special knowledge of one another (Genesis 4:1; 19:8; Numbers 31:17, 35). In many contexts, *yada* denotes the ability to use experience to discern between two alternatives (Genesis 3:5, 22; Deuteronomy 1:39; Isaiah 7:15), an ability that "little ones" lack. Simply put, knowledge is learning with perception. We gain knowledge when we have a teachable spirit, a willingness to listen, and a healthy curiosity. Knowledge forever pursues the truth.

The proverb above says the house is filled with "all precious and pleasant riches," which could be a literal reference to building material wealth. Given the highly symbolic nature of the proverb, however, a figurative interpretation makes more sense. Elsewhere in wisdom literature, riches are the least important pursuit; the priorities of wisdom are, first, obedience to God and, second, harmony with one another. Everything else is a distant third. I suggest, therefore, that those riches are the people of the household.

A practical application of this proverb has to do with relationships. After all, the knowledge gained over time equips family members to deal wisely, reasonably, fairly, and compassionately with one another. We discover one another—our temperaments, aptitudes, strengths, weaknesses, flaws, gifts, and preferences—in order to help one another. Instead of fighting back and taking comments personally, we use the insight gained through experience to respond constructively. Our primary goal is to become responsible agents of God's ways and His plan and to thereby help each member of the household achieve success.

Reflections

How well do you know the other members of your household? I mean *really* know them? For the next week, make a study of each person in turn. Don't focus on the negative; that's obvious and easy. Instead, ask open-ended questions about what they like and don't like, their plans for the future, what causes them fear, what they hope and dream to become. Observe each person in order to discover hidden talents, interests, or skills. Journal your discoveries.

Day 5: *Proverbs 24*
Start Where You Are

With the foundation laid by wisdom, the house built by understanding, and the home filled with knowledge, we have all the ingredients necessary for the cultivation of a happy, prosperous, emotionally safe, spiritually rich household. This is God's ideal for every home, beginning at marriage. Your home, however, may not have started well. Your home may not have incorporated the three essential building materials—wisdom, understanding, and knowledge—and it may have been unhealthy for many years. So you might be asking, *What can be done now?*

I learned a great many years ago that it's never too late to start doing what is right. With God, nothing is ever impossible. Today, we will discuss how those three elements of a good home can help ease the grind of domestic disharmony. As we do so, let me encourage you to think only of your own attitudes and behavior. You can't control other people or compel them to do as God commands, but if you alter your own responses, you will be amazed by the profound effect it may have on others.

1. By wisdom a house is built. (v. 3)

Begin with a personal commitment to know God, study His ways, discover His plan for everyday living, and let this relationship be your guide in all matters. Hopefully, others will join you. If you are married, discuss this with your partner and share your desire to make this commitment an intentional part of your marriage. Regardless of the response you receive, resolve to lay this crucial foundation. This can only improve the emotional climate of your household.

2. By understanding it is established. (v. 3)

The word translated "established" can also mean "set in order." In many contexts, the term expresses the idea of putting something back into an upright position, restoring something that was once leaning, falling, or twisted. In our context, the kind of understanding required involves the practical responsibilities of running a household—providing income, maintaining the assets, keeping everything in working order, and taking reasonable precautions against loss. Everyone should contribute something to the administration of the home, based on ability, of course. Clearly defined responsibilities followed by respectful accountability can do much to reduce interpersonal tension. Resolve to fulfill your own responsibilities without fail and without expecting reward or recognition. Extend to others this same dignity.

3. By knowledge the rooms are filled with all precious and pleasant riches. (v. 4)

When Solomon wrote these words, he used a term that can mean "ever-abundant satisfaction." The constant pursuit of the truth makes that happen. And those "precious and pleasant riches"? Those would be the things that last. To name a few: happy memories; positive and wholesome attitudes; feelings of affirmation, acceptance, and esteem; mutual respect; good relationships; and godly character.

Others—even within your family—might not see the value of this. You do. Without making a show, begin a relentless pursuit of learning about others in your household. Use this knowledge to affirm and encourage whenever possible. Let's face it: in the beginning, you might see a lot more negative than positive. However, harping on the negative has never helped anyone, so make the tiny scraps of positive your focus.

Is your home beginning to deteriorate? Do those living in the home lack a team spirit, a mutual commitment to relationships? Since you cannot force others to change, focus on changing yourself. Begin to demonstrate wisdom, understanding, and knowledge, those three ingredients that can transform a house virtually in shambles into a home of purpose and harmony.

Reflections

What impact on the household do you expect wisdom, understanding, and knowledge to have? Turn this into an experiment. Slowly introduce these elements without explanation and journal the others' responses. Track the progress of the household over several weeks or months.

THE GRIND OF SUBMISSION TO SOVEREIGNTY

The fear of the LORD is the beginning of wisdom,
And the knowledge of the Holy One is understanding.
For by me your days will be multiplied,
And years of life will be added to you.

(Proverbs 9:10–11)

The LORD will not allow the righteous to hunger,
But He will reject the craving of the wicked.

(10:3)

The way of the LORD is a stronghold to the upright,
But ruin to the workers of iniquity.

(10:29)

When a man's ways are pleasing to the LORD,
He makes even his enemies to be at peace with him.

(16:7)

Many plans are in a man's heart,
But the counsel of the LORD will stand.

(19:21)

The king's heart is like channels of water in the hand of the
LORD;
He turns it wherever He wishes.

(21:1)

Day 1: *Proverbs 9, 10, 16, 19, 21*
Divine Right

At first glance this list of Old Testament proverbs may appear like a hodgepodge of random thoughts. A closer look, however, reveals a common theme we tend to overlook or ignore, and that is the theme of God's absolute sovereignty over His creation. By *sovereignty*, I mean God's right as the King of the universe to rule as He sees fit—without question, limitation, accountability, or resistance.

Sovereignty is a difficult concept to grasp in our age of democracy and the rule of law. Earlier civilizations understood the concept of absolute sovereignty all too well. In those days, rulers governed at their own discretion without having to consult anyone, and their decisions were absolute. Kings answered to no one, and the moral code of the land was determined by what they declared right and wrong. When neighbors had a dispute, they took their cases before the king, who then settled the matter by whatever standard he favored—even if that standard changed from day to day based on his mood. His decision was final; his word became law. People trembled before greedy, selfish, ignorant kings and longed for kind, generous, wise rulers.

Of course, the ultimate Sovereign is God. While a human king might be murdered, overthrown, or invaded, God cannot die, and He cannot be unseated from His throne. He answers to no one. His rule is absolute, His decisions permanent. Our moral code—the definition of right and wrong—is determined by His righteous and unchanging character. All must conform to His standard or suffer the consequences of their rebellion. Fortunately, our omnipotent King is good and kind, merciful and patient.

Our troubles begin, however, when our desires conflict with God's and we refuse to acknowledge His sovereignty, His right to rule over His creation.

Reflections

Accepting God's absolute, unquestioned right to rule over you is, ultimately, a matter of trust. Do you trust God? When His will and His way conflict with your own desires, do you trust Him? How difficult do you find it to set aside your own perception and reasoning to give Him the benefit of doubt? How much do you think your human relationships influence your trust in God?

Day 2: *Proverbs 9, 10, 16, 19, 21*

Divine Perspective

Since our generation so admires human ingenuity and worldly wisdom, we tend to give people praise that only God deserves.

- A battle is won—and we hang medals on veterans.
- A degree is earned—and we applaud the graduates.
- A sum of money is donated—and we engrave contributors' names on a plaque.
- An organization stays in the black through hard times—and we grant the CEO a bonus.
- A writer or scientist makes an outstanding contribution—and we award the Pulitzer or a Nobel prize.

- A sermon meets numerous needs—and we praise the preacher.

I certainly don't object to acknowledging and even rewarding excellence. And I see nothing at all wrong with showing appreciation—as long as we acknowledge the One who deserves the ultimate credit and we give Him the greatest glory. Because God works out His will so silently and often mysteriously, His just and loving sovereignty can be easily overlooked, and that's unfortunate. We need a greater awareness and appreciation for God's absolute right to rule His creation as well as His good and perfect reign. Why? Because when we forget God, when we give people too much credit, our view of the world becomes distorted.

Solomon, who was—in human terms—the supreme monarch of Israel, set forth some important truths:

The LORD will not allow the righteous to hunger,
But He will reject the craving of the wicked. (10:3)

The way of the LORD is a stronghold to the upright,
But ruin to the workers of iniquity. (10:29)

Solomon's bottom-line point? God is in charge. Actually, He is the unseen stronghold for the upright, for those who sincerely desire to please God and who submit to His authority. He is a mysterious, invisible obstacle in the way of the wicked, those who willfully reject God's will and intentionally frustrate His plans. But God's sovereign rule is so complete that He will accomplish His objectives and reward the faithful regardless of anyone's opposition.

When a man's ways are pleasing to the LORD,

He makes even his enemies to be at peace with him. (16:7)

God is so powerful that He can honor those who please Him by changing the attitudes of those who once felt enmity toward them. Once all is said and done—after our plans have been hammered out, thought through, reworked, decided on, and distributed—it is His counsel that will ultimately stand.

Reflections

How often do you think about God during a typical day, excluding Sunday? How much does God's Word impact your perspective on your daily duties and interactions? In other words, if the Bible were a pair of tinted lenses, how much does it affect your daily perception of situations and relationships? How would you view the actions of people differently if you saw *everything* as subject to God's administration?

Day 3: *Proverbs 9, 10, 16, 19, 21*

Some Thoughts on Sovereignty

Some people find the concept of God's ultimate and complete sovereignty a little unsettling. Let's face it, we like our autonomy; we find comfort in calling our own shots. Even so, the wise men of Israel, writing under the direction of the Holy Spirit, affirmed God's ultimate authority to administer the world as He sees fit and regardless of human will:

The king's heart is like channels of water in the hand of the
LORD;
He turns it wherever He wishes. (21:1)

This is a comparative couplet: something is compared to something else. Most comparative couplets end with the comparison
and leave it at that, but this proverb concludes with a declarative
statement that offers the reader a timeless principle. Observe the
comparison: "The king's heart is like channels of water in the hand
of the LORD." The Hebrew sentence doesn't begin with "the king's
heart" but rather with "like channels." The Hebrew term translated
"channels" referred to small irrigation ditches running from a main
source—a reservoir—out into dry, thirsty flatlands needing refresh-
ment. In other words: "Like irrigation canals carrying water is the
heart of the king in the LORD's hand."

What's the point? The king's heart—his inner being, the internal part of him that makes decisions—breathes out and communicates attitudes and policies, edicts, and laws. As a result, he may
appear to be in charge, but the entire matter from start to finish
silently and sovereignly rests in the Lord's sovereign hand.

This doctrine of divine sovereignty remains a great theological
controversy and has polarized many scholars. On the one hand, the
doctrine prompts some theologians to nervously reject the idea of
divine sovereignty as "fatalism," a view that all creatures slavishly
follow a preordained script, moving like automatons through life
with only the illusion of choice. Other scholars, however, embrace
and affirm fatalism, calling it "sovereignty." They take the doctrine
of divine sovereignty to unsettling extremes by discounting the vi-
ability of human freedom, suggesting that any amount of human
autonomy compromises God's sovereign rule.

In truth, the Bible affirms both the ultimate sovereignty of God *and* the responsibility of individuals to make wise choices. C. H. Spurgeon was once asked if he could reconcile these two truths. "I wouldn't try," he replied. "I never reconcile friends."[8] God certainly can alter the motivations of an individual who wants to rebel, and He unquestionably has directed the hearts of kings through the ages—Pharaoh (Exodus 10:1–2), Tiglath-Pileser (Isaiah 10:5–7), Cyrus (Isaiah 45:1–6), and Artaxerxes (Ezra 7:21; Nehemiah 2:1–8). Nevertheless, He usually doesn't usurp human will. All activities and events remain under God's ultimate and absolute control, but He grants us varying degrees of freedom to choose our path. The Bible affirms the sovereignty of God over all minutiae of life, yet the Scriptures—especially in the book of Proverbs—continually appeal to our will, urging us to make wise choices.

In the end, regardless of your view of divine sovereignty and human responsibility, you can count on this: each of us will stand before God to account for our decisions, and we must accept the consequences of our choices. On this aspect of God's sovereignty, there is no doubt or debate.

Reflections

God is your King and Judge, but He grants you latitude to make responsible choices. How do you see your freedom in relation to God's sovereignty? How does the reality of God's sovereignty affect the way you make choices? How does your view of God's sovereignty influence the way you pray?

---

8   Charles H. Spurgeon, quoted in *Evangelism and the Sovereignty of God*, J. I. Packer (Downers Grove, IL: InterVarsity Press, 2008), 43.

Day 4: *Proverbs 9, 10, 16, 19, 21*
God-Given Authority

King Nebuchadnezzar enjoyed the kind of power and privilege no single human had ever experienced. He built an empire that eventually swallowed two other great civilizations, Assyria and Egypt. At the time, no one man controlled more of the world than he. According to the man's written testimony, Nebuchadnezzar became intoxicated by his own wealth and power. His position as the most powerful man on earth gave him a skewed perspective on life and the world.

> [Nebuchadnezzar] was walking on the roof of the royal palace of Babylon. The king reflected and said, "Is this not Babylon the great, which I myself have built as a royal residence by the might of my power and for the glory of my majesty?" While the word was in the king's mouth, a voice came from heaven, saying, "King Nebuchadnezzar, to you it is declared: sovereignty has been removed from you, and you will be driven away from mankind, and your dwelling place will be with the beasts of the field. You will be given grass to eat like cattle, and seven periods of time will pass over you until you recognize that the Most High is ruler over the realm of mankind and bestows it on whomever He wishes." Immediately the word concerning Nebuchadnezzar was fulfilled. (Daniel 4:29–33)

For an extended period of time, the great king suffered a mental condition called lycanthropy, which drove him to behave like a wild animal. No longer walking proudly on the ramparts of his accomplishments, he now shuffled along like a beast. At the end of his ordeal, the king wrote:

At the end of that period, I, Nebuchadnezzar, raised my eyes toward heaven and my reason returned to me, and I blessed the Most High and praised and honored Him who lives forever;

> For His dominion is an everlasting dominion,
> And His kingdom endures from generation to generation.
> All the inhabitants of the earth are accounted as nothing,
> But He does according to His will in the host of heaven
> And among the inhabitants of earth;
> And no one can ward off His hand
> Or say to Him, "What have You done?" (Daniel 4:34–35)

Reflections

You have undoubtedly been granted some sovereignty in a particular realm of life, such as a department at work, your home, etc. What did you do to merit this position? How much of your identity or sense of worth is tied to your accomplishments? How do your power and privilege impact your relationship with God?

Day 5: *Proverbs 9, 10, 16, 19, 21*

Submitting As We Serve

> He does according to His will in the host of heaven
> And among the inhabitants of earth;
> And no one can ward off His hand
> Or say to Him, "What have You done?" (Daniel 4:35)

Those are the words of a powerful king—the richest, most powerful man in the world at the time—and he is describing God's sovereignty soon after his encounter with humility. Nebuchadnezzar had built an empire and conquered much of the ancient world. His word became law for millions of people. He could do virtually anything he desired. He answered to no man, no political party, no constituency, no institution. After the Lord worked him over, however, the earthly king who ruled over kings discovered a power greater than his own. The greatest sovereign on earth realized he was a helpless creature before the sovereign King of heaven.

What is true of Nebuchadnezzar and all kings who followed in his footsteps remains true today. Politicians, kings, tyrants, dictators, presidents, managers, supervisors, pastors, elders, deacons—leaders small and great—all must recognize that they are subject to the ultimate sovereignty of God. Whether rulers like it or not, accept it or live in rebellion, regardless, God will ultimately have His way. A position of privilege, power, or authority demands wise, humble stewardship. Because God gave you the gift of autonomy—a degree of latitude in making decisions—you may choose to challenge His authority or attempt to resist His sovereign will, but I've got news for you—God has never met His match. He will win. He will have His way. So if you face a high-stress day and submitting to your sovereign Lord doesn't seem all that proactive or productive, take my advice: do it anyway. You'll be glad later. Maybe sooner.

Whenever you submit, whenever you place yourself under the sovereign God's authority, seek His will, and discover His way, you make yourself His ally. As the sages of Israel wrote many centuries ago,

> All the ways of a man are clean in his own sight,
> But the LORD weighs the motives.
> Commit your works to the LORD
> And your plans will be established. (Proverbs 16:2–3)

Reflections

What positions of privilege, power, or authority do you currently hold? In what contexts must other people follow your lead? (Don't forget family!) What is the purpose of each organization or group? How can its purpose serve the overall plan of God for the world? How does this divine possibility change your perspective as a leader in that organization?

THE GRIND OF LAZINESS

The hand of the diligent will rule,
But the slack hand will be put to forced labor.

(Proverbs 12:24)

A lazy man does not roast his prey,
But the precious possession of a man is diligence.

(12:27)

The soul of the sluggard craves and gets nothing,
But the soul of the diligent is made fat.

(13:4)

The way of the lazy is as a hedge of thorns,
But the path of the upright is a highway.

(15:19)

He also who is slack in his work
Is brother to him who destroys.

(18:9)

Laziness casts into a deep sleep,
And an idle man will suffer hunger.

(19:15)

The sluggard says, "There is a lion outside;
I will be killed in the streets!"

(22:13)

The sluggard says, "There is a lion in the road!
A lion is in the open square!"
As the door turns on its hinges,
So does the sluggard on his bed.
The sluggard buries his hand in the dish;
He is weary of bringing it to his mouth again.
The sluggard is wiser in his own eyes
Than seven men who can give a discreet answer.

(26:13–16)

Day I: *Proverbs 12, 13, 15, 18, 19, 22, 26*

The Gift of Labor

Many people live under the impression that work is a curse. Some even attempt to quote Scripture to support their position that work is the sad consequence of Adam's fall in the garden of Eden. Wrong! Before sin ever entered the world, before Adam's disobedience subjected the world to the consequences of sin, and when total innocence still prevailed, God assigned humanity the task of cultivating the garden, filling the world, and ruling over the earth (Genesis 1:28; 2:15).

Labor is not a curse. On the contrary, it is a gift from God. He gave humanity the honor of becoming His vice-regents over the earth. The fall of humanity, however, transformed work into toil. When God confronted Adam, whom He held responsible for the couple's sin, God pronounced several curses. One such pronouncement concerned the ground:

Then to Adam He said, "Because you have listened to the voice of your wife, and have eaten from the tree about which I commanded you, saying, 'You shall not eat from it';
Cursed is the ground because of you;
In toil you will eat of it
All the days of your life.
Both thorns and thistles it shall grow for you;
And you will eat the plants of the field;
By the sweat of your face
You will eat bread,
Till you return to the ground,
Because from it you were taken;
For you are dust,
And to dust you shall return." (Genesis 3:17–19)

The English term *curse* is far too tame a rendering of the Hebrew verb *arar*, which means "to bind (with a spell), hem in with obstacles, render powerless to resist."[9] God warned Adam and Eve that disobedience would bring about death, that sin would result in unwanted consequences. When they disobeyed, creation began the long, slow, agonizing death that continues today (Romans 8:19–22). The world became twisted, order became disorganized, relationships suffered strife, and work became toil. Whereas God created the earth to respond to the cultivating hand of humanity, now everything resists our subduing. If weeds don't choke out our crops, pests try to eat them before the harvest.

The curse that followed the fall is also behind the hassles—the thorn-and-thistle-like irritations—that now frustrate one's work. Work itself is a privilege. It is also a challenge to indolence, an answer to boredom, an opportunity for personal growth and

---

9   Victor P. Hamilton, "168 *arar*," in *Theological Wordbook of the Old Testament*, ed. R. Laird Harris, Gleason L. Archer Jr. and Bruce K. Waltke, (Chicago: Moody Press, 1999), 75.

development, and a worthy place to invest one's energy. And, perhaps most important of all, work provides for our physical needs.

Reflections

What do you see as the primary difference between work and drudgery? What work do you find most fulfilling? How does God use your current occupation to develop you as a person? How can you cooperate with His development program?

Day 2: *Proverbs 12, 13, 15, 18, 19, 22, 26*

Overcoming Inertia

Throughout the Bible we are encouraged to be people of diligence, committed to the tasks in life that we need to accomplish. Some, however, do not consider this a privilege, but a burden. For those folks the daily grind of laziness is an undeniable reality. For this entire week, we'll take a close-up look at this practical plague.

Of all the Scriptures that address the issue of laziness, none are more eloquent than the sayings of Solomon. Among the terms he used for the lazy, *sluggard* appears to be his favorite. When I trace my way through the Proverbs, I find six characteristics of the sluggard. Over the next few days, we'll examine them together and determine ways to avoid the sluggard's errors.

1. The sluggard has trouble getting started.

How long will you lie down, O sluggard?
When will you arise from your sleep?

"A little sleep, a little slumber,
A little folding of the hands to rest"—
Your poverty will come in like a vagabond
And your need like an armed man. (6:9–11)

You may remember this passage from our discussion of the grind of procrastination. (It might be worth reviewing Week 12 before reading on.) There is no getting around it: laziness focuses on the obstacles, the excuses that loom large on the front end of a task. Those who are lazy just can't seem to roll up their sleeves and plunge in.

In addition to the already mentioned causes of procrastination, I would add this: the size of a task can often be daunting. Nothing can stop me in my tracks faster than feeling overwhelmed. Just thinking about all the details and the immense effort the job requires is exhausting. I would rather lie down for "a little sleep, a little slumber." To ease this grind, I find it helpful to break the job down into manageable pieces, and I make the first portion of the job relatively easy to accomplish. Doing this helps me get started. If I can overcome the inertia and begin tackling a difficult project, the momentum I gain helps me continue.

At other times, I find it hard to start a large project because I'm not sure where to begin. I worry that doing things out of order will create more work, making the already difficult job harder to complete. If I dawdle around too long, however, "poverty will come in like a vagabond," so I can't do nothing forever. Sometimes, I've found, it's best to simply jump in and start working. Inevitably, I quickly get a good sense of where I should have begun and a plan quickly unfolds in my mind. I might have wasted some effort, but at least the project is under way.

Reflections

Think of a daunting project or an unpleasant task you would prefer to avoid. Break the job down into small tasks you can accomplish in one day or less and write those tasks on a calendar. Post the calendar where others can see your plan and view your progress. Trust me: this accountability will help.

Day 3: *Proverbs 12, 13, 15, 18, 19, 22, 26*

Big Talk

Solomon and the wise men of Israel identified six characteristics of a sluggard. Our responsibility is to identify these faulty traits, examine ourselves to see if they have taken root in us, and then counter them with specific behaviors that teach us how to be diligent and faithful in our responsibilities. According to the book of Proverbs,

2. The sluggard is restless: He (or she) may have desires, but the trouble comes in implementing them.

The soul of the sluggard craves and gets nothing,
But the soul of the diligent is made fat. (13:4)

The desire of the sluggard puts him to death,
For his hands refuse to work;
All day long he is craving,
While the righteous gives and does not hold back. (21:25–26)

It is not uncommon for lazy people to be extremely skilled and very creative individuals who possess great potential. They can talk and dream and even sketch out the game plan, but they lack the discipline to pursue their vision. As we just read, their "craving" goes on "all day long," but little gets accomplished. When pressed for an explanation, their excuses bear witness to their creativity as well as to their unwillingness to apply themselves.

In my observation of people over the years, this kind of laziness results from one of three possible faults:

Lack of Confidence

A profound sense of doubt in one's own capabilities can be coupled with a fear of exposing this incompetence. In truth, everyone lacks to some degree the confidence to attempt something new or untried. We all take on new challenges wondering if we have what it takes to see the job through to the end. Those who do not want to become sluggards choose to forge ahead with the expectation that, as they try, fail, assess, and grow, they will develop the skills necessary to succeed.

Lack of Skill

Sluggards won't apply themselves without complete assurance at the beginning that they will not fail. If they lack the necessary skills, they console themselves with pipe dreams and petty assurances they could have succeeded "if only." Those who do not want to become sluggards recognize their own lack of qualifications, but they decide to acquire the skills they need to accomplish their goals.

Lack of Desire

Sluggards are complacent people—and don't mistake contentment for complacency. Unlike people who are content with what they have, sluggards feel entitled to greater wealth and more possessions, but they remain unwilling to do what is necessary to acquire them. People who are content feel gratified by what they accomplish regardless of the material reward. Sluggards want the rewards of hard work without putting forth the effort.

> The sluggard buries his hand in the dish;
> He is weary of bringing it to his mouth again. (26:15)

To avoid the sluggard's sense of entitlement, pursue worthy goals without regard for wealth or possessions. Invest yourself in something meaningful and derive satisfaction from accomplishments that honor God.

Reflections

Setting aside considerations of wealth or even sustenance, what goals or objectives that align with God's agenda appeal to you? What keeps you from pursuing one or more of these dreams? Perhaps you should adjust your prayers: give God the responsibility to sustain you and ask for His help in pursuing a God-honoring goal, objective, or vocation.

Day 4: *Proverbs 12, 13, 15, 18, 19, 22, 26*
All Take, No Give

In our study of what the book of Proverbs says about laziness, we have discovered two unpleasant character traits common to sluggards. We have also considered practical ways to address these flaws. Today, we learn how a prototypical lazy person handles relationships. (You have undoubtedly seen these characteristics in others. Maybe you've been guilty at times?)

3. The sluggard takes a costly toll on others.

He also who is slack in his work
Is brother to him who destroys. (18:9)

As John Donne wrote, "No man is an island entire of itself . . . [and] any man's death diminishes me."[10] This could well be rendered "No one is an island entire of itself, and anyone's *laziness* diminishes me." So much of what we try to accomplish as individuals depends on the efforts of others. When one person fails to pay a bill, everyone in the family is affected. When one team member slacks off, the others must add that person's work to the list of their own responsibilities. A lazy employee doesn't simply hold an organization back, but also undermines coworkers' motivation and drive. A lazy player doesn't merely weaken the team, but also saps its spirit and deflates its confidence. A lazy pastor doesn't merely limit a church, but also undercuts its passion. Before long, everyone must do more to compensate for a sluggard's negative influence.

And if that weren't difficult enough . . .

4. The sluggard is usually defensive.
The sluggard is wiser in his own eyes
Than seven men who can give a discreet answer. (26:16)

You have undoubtedly heard the infinite creativity of a lazy person's rationalizing. This can be seen quite often in a game called "You Can't Solve My Problem." For every suggestion made, the

---

10 John Donne, *The Works of John Donne, D.D.: With a Memoir of His Life*, Vol. III, ed. Henry Alford (London: John W. Parker, West Strand, 1839), 575.

sluggard always has a reason why that won't work, a credible argument as to why that solution will not help. Unfortunately, this clever ability to cover up or explain away keeps the lazy person from coming to terms with reality.

Let's face facts. We've all been guilty of this at one time or another, and all of us will likely face this temptation again. So, what's the solution if you find yourself playing the part of a sluggard? In a word: *selflessness*. Laziness is selfish thinking. Get over yourself, think about the people around you, empathize with their struggles. Doing your job well is a great way to ease other people's burdens. If completing your tasks brings no personal satisfaction, be satisfied that your diligence benefits others.

Reflections

When you fail to follow through on your duties, who is affected and what is the impact? Which of your responsibilities, when done well and on time, makes life better for the greatest number of people? When establishing priorities, let this selflessness add a new dimension to your planning.

Day 5: *Proverbs 12, 13, 15, 18, 19, 22, 26*
No Follow-Through

A young fellow entered a convenience store and asked to use the phone. The manager overheard his side of the conversation as he asked, "Sir, could you use a hardworking, honest young man to work for you?" (pause) "Oh, you've already got a hardworking, honest young man? Well, thanks anyway!"

The boy hung up the phone with a smile and turned to leave, humming a happy tune.

"How can you be so cheery?" asked the eavesdropping manager. "I thought the man you talked to already had someone and didn't want to hire you."

The young fellow answered, "Well, you see, *I am* the hardworking young man. I was just checking up on my job!"

If someone asked your boss about your position and your performance, what do you think the response would be? Would your boss say you are hardworking? Not if you have these two final attributes of a lazy person:

5. *The sluggard is a quitter.*
A lazy man does not roast his prey,
But the precious possession of a man is diligence. (12:27)

This colorful saying reveals another telltale mark of laziness: a lack of thoroughness. The lazy person:

- Likes to catch fish, but doesn't clean them.
- Loves to eat, but hates doing the dishes.
- Doesn't mind painting a room, but leaves the cleanup to others.
- Prefers nice possessions, but fails to care for them properly.

Sluggards can't be bothered with details because they're satisfied with the bare minimum. Excellence ranks low on their list of priorities.

6. The sluggard lives by excuses.

The sluggard says, "There is a lion outside;
I will be killed in the streets!" (22:13)

This saying always makes me smile. Those lions in the street are nothing more than a fertile imagination gone to seed. Later in the book of Proverbs, the "lion"' returns:

The sluggard says, "There is a lion in the road!
A lion is in the open square!"
As the door turns on its hinges,
So does the sluggard on his bed. (26:13–14)

These proverbs use a figure of speech called hyperbole, a humorous, outrageous image that illustrates a valid point. The first hyperbole demonstrates the ridiculous lengths to which a lazy person will go to avoid work. The sluggard will capitalize on any excuse, no matter how unlikely or irrational. The second proverb illustrates the only possible result of the lazy person's nature. Bound by hinges, a door has a limited range of motion: a door can do nothing else but swing open and shut. So also the lazy person: a sluggard's nature allows no action beyond the bed.

Reflections

Do you happen to have a lazy acquaintance who holds you and others back? Frequently, an unhealthy or unwholesome association gives us just the excuse we need to settle for too many limitations. Reflect on the kinds of people with whom you spend most of your time. When possible, choose diligent friends and limit your exposure to people exhibiting the traits of a sluggard.

The Grind of Imbalance

If you are slack in the day of distress,
Your strength is limited.

(Proverbs 24:10)

Two things I asked of You,
Do not refuse me before I die:
Keep deception and lies far from me,
Give me neither poverty nor riches;
Feed me with the food that is my portion,
That I not be full and deny You and say, "Who is the Lord?"
Or that I not be in want and steal,
And profane the name of my God.

(30:7–9)

Day 1: *Proverbs 24*
Unbalanced

The longer I live, the more I realize how easily a routine can become a rut and how quickly priorities can become obsessions. Last week we examined the grind of laziness and discovered ways to avoid becoming a sluggard. But the decision to make work a priority and be diligent in our responsibilities can carry us to extremes: our industriousness can become workaholism.

In terms of diet, we monitor what we eat and how much, and doctors recommend we work up a good sweat on a regular basis. Some, however, take health consciousness to such lengths that they suffer from eating disorders. Some women work out so much that their female hormones shut down, and some men feel the need to inject themselves with muscle-building compounds that cause cancer. These are examples of good things—concern about eating and exercising wisely—made bad by taking them to extremes.

In the same way, I've seen Christians take spiritual disciplines to such extremes that they all but withdrew from normal public life. They take Paul's admonition to "pray without ceasing" literally and spend hours in private meditation and accomplish very little else. They study Scripture so long and so deeply that they have little opportunity to live out what they have learned. They attend every church service, participate in every church program, and never miss a single church event—and their children feel ignored and their marriage partner is neglected. Again, good things made bad when we fail to find an appropriate balance.

I see imbalance and extremes all around me, and sometimes— to my own embarrassment—in myself. A major prayer of mine as I grow older is "Lord, keep me balanced!"

- We need a balance between work and play. Too much of either is unhealthy and distasteful.
- We need a balance between time alone and time with others. Too much of either takes a personal toll.
- We need a balance between independence and dependence. Too much of either one leads to bizarre behavior and even mental disorders.
- We need a balance between kindness and firmness, between waiting and praying, between working and obeying,

between saving and spending, between taking in and giving out, between wanting too much and expecting too little, between gracious acceptance and keen discernment.

Reflections

Examine your own life. In what area of life might you need more balance? Now reflect on the past few weeks. Has anyone close to you complained about your taking some activity, priority, or perspective to an extreme?

Day 2: *Proverbs 24*

Adversity versus Prosperity

Whether or not you realize it, life is a perpetual struggle to maintain balance between various opposing forces. Over the next few days, we will examine some common extremes that threaten to pull us off balance. The first is the tug-of-war between adversity and prosperity.

When reflecting on the effects of adversity, the sages of Israel wrote,

> If you are slack in the day of distress,
> Your strength is limited. (24:10)

The term rendered "distress" is a word picture describing confinement or constriction, a place too small to inhabit comfortably. The expression "between a rock and a hard place" is fitting. This proverb counsels against our "becoming slack" or, more precisely, "idle, disheartened, dropped down, slumped." If we do, we sacrifice strength that would normally help us escape. In other words, when we give in to our fears, we allow what we fear to become reality. And, according to Proverbs 24:5, "A wise man is strong; and a man of knowledge increases power."

To put it bluntly, giving up is stupid!

When adversity pins us down, let survival be our primary goal. Don't even entertain the idea of giving up. Instead, let adversity put our resiliency and creativity to the test. Adversity demands that we reach deep down into our inner character and gut out a solution. Very often, the Lord uses adversity to help us recognize a reservoir of inner strength.

We face a far more subtle test, however, when we encounter prosperity, the opposite of adversity. When things come easily, when there's plenty of money, when everybody applauds, when all our ducks line up in a neat row, when the sky's the limit, that's the time to hang tough! Why? Because in times of prosperity, life can become subtly complicated. Integrity comes under attack. Humility is put to the test. Faith is challenged. Proverbs warns,

> He who trusts in his riches will fall,
> But the righteous will flourish like the green leaf. (11:28)

The word rendered "trusts" means "to feel secure, to have confidence, to depend upon." When we're suffering adversity, we naturally become introspective, carefully monitoring our motives and decisions to satisfy ourselves that we do not deserve our unpleasant circumstances. We tend to become less concerned about our behavior when life is going well, and if we're not careful, we can begin to feel indestructible. Our prosperity feels like a shield from calamity. We might even mistake our wealth as proof of God's affirmation and develop a sense of entitlement.

Wisdom tells us to focus not on our circumstances—adversity or prosperity—but to find balance in doing what is right. The "righteous" in 11:28 refers to those who consistently follow and apply God's moral standards regardless of circumstances.

Reflections

If you are like most people, your life is a mixture of both adversity and prosperity, depending on which particular situation you consider. Compile two lists: ways in which you suffer adversity *and* ways in which you are prosperous. How are you tempted to give up righteous behavior in each circumstance? Resolve now to do what is right in response to each temptation.

Day 3: *Proverbs 24*
Work versus Reward

As we discovered earlier, Solomon and the wise men of Israel had a lot to say about the value of diligence and the dangers of laziness. When we put all the sayings together, their message becomes clear: work diligently and you will reap material rewards; laziness will leave you penniless. Even in this, however, the proverbs call for balance. In favor of work, the wise men wrote:

A worker's appetite works for him,
For his hunger urges him on. (16:26)

The word translated "appetite" is the Hebrew term for "soul." In this context, it refers to the human desire to meet our basic needs for survival. Literally, a person must have water, food, and shelter. This biological need drives us to work. In a broader sense of the expression, the sage acknowledged our spiritual need for meaningful work. God designed us with this "hunger," and we reflect His image when we fulfill our divine purpose (Genesis 1:28; 2:15).

This need, however, can become an obsession. Hunger urges us to work, but greed—or one of many personal issues—compels us to work too much. God calls us to diligence, but He doesn't want workaholics. According to this book of wisdom, there is both a time to work and a time to enjoy the fruit of our labor.

> Prepare your work outside
> And make it ready for yourself in the field;
> Afterwards, then, build your house. (24:27)

The phrase *build your house* has both a literal and a figurative meaning. To build one's house, a man not only erected a structure in which to live, but he worked to establish a legacy. He married, filled the home with children, reared them to adulthood, and then enlarged the dwelling to accommodate the next generation. In this sense, a person's house represented his life, which he filled with family, friends, wealth, and provisions for security.

To paraphrase this proverb, "Work hard! Then, get a life!"

Reflections

Which extreme do you tend to overindulge—the *process* of work or the *reward* of work? What might you do to maintain a healthier balance? In what ways can you involve family and friends in helping you maintain balance?

Day 4: *Proverbs 24*
Wisdom, Understanding, and Knowledge

Solomon and the wise men of Israel regarded wisdom, understanding, and knowledge as worthy pursuits in life. In fact, given the choice between wisdom and material wealth, they opted for wisdom, hands down. For them, clear thinking held the key to success in all areas of life.

> How much better it is to get wisdom than gold!
> And to get understanding is to be chosen above silver.
> (16:16)

> Discretion will guard you,
> Understanding will watch over you. (2:11)

> The lips of the righteous feed many,
> But fools die for lack of understanding. (10:21)

> Understanding is a fountain of life to one who has it,
> But the discipline of fools is folly. (16:22)

Let's review the definitions of *wisdom*, *understanding*, and *knowledge*.

For the Hebrews, *wisdom* (*hakam*) and its derivatives are the most commonly used terms denoting intelligence. This kind of wisdom describes perception with discernment. The original Hebrew word emphasizes accuracy and the ability to sense what is beneath the surface. This virtue represents a manner of thinking and an attitude that result in prudent, sensible living. "The wisdom of the OT, however, is quite distinct from other ancient world views. . . . Reflected in OT wisdom is the teaching of a personal God who is holy and just and who expects those who know him to exhibit his character in the many practical affairs of life."[11]

The Hebrew term for "understanding" is *tebuna*, which denotes intelligence or discernment. This word describes our ability to observe, gain insight, and then discern in order to devise a plan or make a decision. To gain this kind of mental capability, we do our homework, investigate, seek multiple perspectives, use logic, and formulate ideas. We might call this "experiential wisdom," the kind of savvy that older people gain from the school of hard knocks.

The Hebrew term for *knowledge* is based on the verb *yada*, "to know." This is understanding with insight. This kind of knowledge is based on personal experience with a matter. The Bible uses this of God's all-knowing familiarity with each individual and his or her mannerisms (Genesis 18:19; Deuteronomy 34:10; Isaiah 48:8; Psalms 1:6; 37:18). In many contexts, it denotes the ability to discern, based on past experience, the difference between two things (Genesis 3:5, 22; Deuteronomy 1:39; Isaiah 7:15), an ability that "little ones" lack. Knowledge, therefore, is learning with perception. It includes things like a teachable spirit, a willingness to listen, a desire to discover what is really there. Knowledge forever pursues the truth.

Solomon and the wise men of Israel prized wisdom, understanding, and knowledge as crucial to living prosperously, safely, and effectively. Even so, they recognized the limits of human thinking:

---

11 Louis Goldberg, "647 *hakam*," in *Theological Wordbook of the Old Testament*, ed. R. Laird Harris, Gleason L. Archer Jr. and Bruce K. Waltke, electronic ed. (Chicago: Moody Press, 1999), 283.

Trust in the LORD with all your heart
And do not lean on your own understanding.
In all your ways acknowledge Him,
And He will make your paths straight.
Do not be wise in your own eyes;
Fear the LORD and turn away from evil. (3:5–7)

Reflections

How have you invested in your own education so far? What will you
do to continue to cultivate—in the Hebrew sense of those words—
wisdom, understanding, and knowledge? When approaching a challenge, how do you employ both human wisdom and trust in God?
In what do you ultimately trust?

Day 5: *Proverbs 24*
Prosperity: Not Too Little, Not Too Much

As we conclude our examination of balance or the lack of it,
let's return to where we started. A wise man of Israel reflected on his wealth and its effect on his relationship with God. He
then formulated this prayer asking the Lord to help him maintain
a wise balance:

Two things I asked of You,
Do not refuse me before I die:
Keep deception and lies far from me,
Give me neither poverty nor riches;
Feed me with the food that is my portion,

That I not be full and deny You and say, "Who is the LORD?"
Or that I not be in want and steal,
And profane the name of my God. (30:7–9)

This man had lived enough years and experienced sufficient challenges to boil his petition down to two specifics:

1. Keep me from deception and liars.
2. Give me neither too little nor too much prosperity.

It is the second request that helps him maintain a proper balance. That is the one he amplified. Why did he resist having too little? He wanted to avoid any temptation to meet his needs through dishonest means. Desperate people do desperate things. Whoever doubts that has never looked into the faces of his or her starving children. At that moment, feeding them could easily overrule upholding some high-and-mighty principle. Adversity can tempt us to profane the name of our God.

And why did the writer fear possessing too much? When we're fat-'n'-sassy, we're most vulnerable to both pride and the temptation to forget God. That's when we risk becoming like Nebuchadnezzar, who credited himself for his success. That's when we place greater trust in our wealth to provide for our needs and to give us security. Prosperity can tempt us to presume on the grace of God.

Think it over. The adversary of our souls is the expert of extremes. He never runs out of ways to push us to the limit, to get us so far out to one extreme that we risk a serious moral tumble. The longer I live, the more I must fight the tendency to go to extremes, and the more I value balance.

Reflections

Let's do a little honest appraisal, okay? To help keep your appraisal on a fairly reliable footing, you need these two things:

a. Your calendar
b. Your bank statements

Look through your calendar over the last thirty days. Then, as best you can, fill in the typical days of a typical week with your activities. Do you see any extremes? Do you see anything missing, such as time with family, time devoted to serving God, or time set aside for rest and recreation?

Now look through your bank statements. Do your expenditures reflect balance or imbalance? Do you spend too much or not enough on yourself? How about God's part of your income? Do you see any extremes? Do you see something missing?

THE GRIND OF OPPOSITION

Wisdom shouts in the street,
She lifts her voice in the square;
At the head of the noisy streets she cries out;
At the entrance of the gates in the city she utters her sayings:
"How long, O naive ones, will you love being simple-minded?
And scoffers delight themselves in scoffing
And fools hate knowledge?"

(Proverbs 1:20–22)

They hated knowledge
And did not choose the fear of the LORD.
"They would not accept my counsel,
They spurned all my reproof.
"So they shall eat of the fruit of their own way
And be satiated with their own devices.
"For the waywardness of the naive will kill them,
And the complacency of fools will destroy them."

(1:29–32)

Day 1: *Proverbs 1*
The Greater of Two Evils

What did you first envision when you saw the word *opposition* in the chapter title? Did you imagine external resistance to your efforts or your own internal resistance to God's leading? Which do you think would be the greater "grind"?

By *opposition*, I don't refer to external resistance from others but to internal resistance, to our own opposition to the things of God. In truth, our encounters with external forces—with people and circumstances that frustrate our efforts—are not likely to destroy us. What I have in mind is how we personally resist God's leading, His reproofs, His will, His wisdom. Some are so given to internal opposition that they regularly fail to learn the lessons the Spirit of Truth attempts to teach. While others glean God's message and follow His principles, many spurn His ways.

All of us, at one time or another, become guilty of internal opposition. We must then ask ourselves two important questions:

How often do we resist God's working within us?
Does our resistance threaten to become habitual?

These are crucial questions, and your answers will determine how your future will unfold in the realm of time and space as well as in eternity beyond death. You see, God is in the business of redeeming and transforming people. While the Bible affirms that He will not fail to accomplish what He determines to do, the Bible also appeals to the will of each individual, calling each of us to heed the voice of wisdom, to repent of our rebellion, to seek God's direction, and to submit to His leading.

Reflections

Have you made the decision to follow God's leading in every detail of your life? No one does this perfectly. But as a matter of life orientation, do you resolve to do things God's way, according to His will, His methods, and His timing? If not, why are you opposed to that? What do you fear most? I urge you to cease resisting; now is a good time to commit yourself to following God's leading.

Day 2: *Proverbs 1*
Simple Opposition

As a pastor, I have been amazed at the difference among Christians when it comes to accepting instruction. Some *never* seem to learn! Many believers remain keenly aware of God's leading, submitting to every nuance of His internal prompting, but many other churchgoing followers of Christ insist on learning the hard way. They are exposed to the same truths year after year, but wisdom fails to soak in. Multiple warnings from family and friends go unheeded. Brushes with disaster fail to alter their course. Even as they sit in the rubble of sin's consequences, they typically ask, "How did this happen? Why am I suffering?"

When I came across three types of individuals in Scripture, I began to understand these people struggle with a common problem. They are people of opposition; they oppose God's instruction. These rebels come in three varieties, each described in Proverbs by Solomon and his fellow wise men. We will examine each of these three over the next few days.

Wise King Solomon called the first opposing group "the simple-minded."

The Simple-Minded

The Hebrew noun *peti* is based on a verb that means "to be spacious, open, wide." It carries the idea of being completely open, undiscerning, unable or unwilling to distinguish between truth and falsehood; of being easily misled, quickly enticed, and easily falling prey to deception. The naive are susceptible to evil and easily influenced by any opinion. They are usually unable to cope with life's complexities, especially if the situation requires a great deal of mental effort.

In Hebrew culture, children are expected to be simple-minded. They lack the education, experience, and training to be discerning. Therefore, parents had the sacred duty to protect naive young ones from deception and to equip them for adulthood. Few tolerated simple-minded adults, however. Except in cases of mental impairment, adults remained naive by choice and therefore deserved to suffer the consequences of their simple-mindedness.

Reading through Proverbs, I found several traits of the simple:

- They are insensitive to danger or evil.

I looked out through my lattice,
And I saw among the naive,
And discerned among the youths
A young man lacking sense,
Passing through the street near [the harlot's] corner;
And he takes the way to her house,
In the twilight, in the evening,
In the middle of the night and in the darkness.

Suddenly he follows her
As an ox goes to the slaughter. (7:6–9, 22)

* They do not foresee or even consider the consequences
  of their decisions.

"Whoever is naive, let him turn in here,"
And to him who lacks understanding she says,
"Stolen water is sweet;
And bread eaten in secret is pleasant."
But he does not know that the dead are there,
That her guests are in the depths of Sheol. (9:16–18)

* They are gullible; they lack discernment.

The naive believes everything,
But the sensible man considers his steps. (14:15)

* They fail to learn; they plunge in again and again!

The prudent sees the evil and hides himself,
But the naive go on, and are punished for it. (22:3)

Reflections

There's an old saying: "Fool me once, shame on you; fool me twice, shame on me!" How well do you learn from your mistakes? Are you able to see the connection between your decisions and the consequences of those decisions? Self-condemnation is not the goal, but a careful examination of past suffering will often reveal some personal responsibility. How well do you engage in this mature discipline?

Day 3: *Proverbs 1*

Stupid Opposition

Hebrew culture recognized that not all opposition to God's leading is the same. All opposition is foolishness, but the Old Testament sages diagnosed the different root causes of spiritual stupidity and addressed them accordingly. Yesterday, we examined simple foolishness, the opposition of those who simply have not learned, of people who have not been trained. Today, we consider a more severe form of spiritual foolishness, a condition that might be called "stupid opposition." The best English term for this person is *fool*.

The Fool

The Hebrew language has two primary terms for this kind of fool: *nabal* and *kasal*. Both have the basic meaning "to be stupid, dull." Arabic has a term similar to *kasal* that means "to be sluggish, thick, coarse." Don't misunderstand. The fool has the *capacity* to reason; he simply applies logic incorrectly. Fools are absolutely convinced they can get along quite well without God. Fools fashion for themselves a rationale that creates the *appearance* of honest logic. In truth, however, they begin with their desired conclusions and then support them with rationalizations.

A good example of *kasal* might be a man who suffers a terrible, tragic loss, becomes intensely angry with God, and then decides the Creator doesn't exist. He then spends his life building a logical case against the existence of God using what appears to be credible reasoning. To further convince himself and others as well, he proposes alternate theories of how and why the universe exists in order to replace a biblical worldview.

In truth, atheism is simply a modern form of idolatry—a willful rejection of God in favor of a man-made cosmos. Perhaps this is why the Bible uses *kasal* most often for idolaters: these people create for themselves an idol and then convince themselves it has supernatural power. The prophet Isaiah illustrated this absurdity in the tale of a man who cut down a tree:

> Half of it he burns in the fire; over this half he eats meat as he roasts a roast and is satisfied. He also warms himself and says, "Aha! I am warm, I have seen the fire." But the rest of it he makes into a god, his graven image. He falls down before it and worships; he also prays to it and says, "Deliver me, for you are my god." (Isaiah 44:16–17)

In similar fashion, a *nabal* decides what kind of sinful behavior he most enjoys and then rationalizes it. A woman preparing to leave her family for the sake of an affair will, for instance, spend many weeks mentally preparing herself for the break. She'll convince herself that her husband and family are better off without her, that she has served others long enough and now it's her time to enjoy life, or that the other man is her true soul mate and that God would want her to be happy.

Do you see the correlation? Most modern people don't create statues to venerate as gods. Instead, people today decide what they want to believe and then rationalize their decision with no consideration for the fact they have placed their trust in lies of their own making! Scripture rebukes this kind of opposition in the sharpest of terms and offers wise people a specific response to the folly of fools.

Leave the presence of a fool,
Or you will not discern words of knowledge.
The wisdom of the sensible is to understand his way,
But the foolishness of fools is deceit. (14:7–8)

The mind of the intelligent seeks knowledge,
But the mouth of fools feeds on folly. (15:14)

A fool does not delight in understanding,
But only in revealing his own mind. (18:2)

He who trusts in his own heart is a fool,
But he who walks wisely will be delivered. (28:26)

Reflections

It is possible for even wise people to play the fool in some respects. When have you been guilty of rationalizing behavior you knew was contrary to God's will? Why did you protect that behavior so carefully? What need or desire does this behavior satisfy for you? Consider presenting that need to God, asking Him to provide satisfaction in His way and according to His timing.

Day 4: *Proverbs 1*

Willful Opposition

Of the three distinct types of rebel—those who oppose God's internal leading and instruction—the simple-minded or naive bear the least moral guilt. Children are expected to be simple-minded, but they come to bear greater responsibility for their naiveté as they grow older. Still, their failure to learn from the school of hard knocks is less sinful than those who scoff at God's direction. The Bible reserves its most severe rebuke for this kind of opposition.

The Scoffer

This person is quite different from the simple one. The scoffer "delights in his scoffing." The Hebrew term *lūtz* means "to turn aside, to scorn, to mock." It expresses the idea of rejecting with vigorous contempt. Scoffers show disdain or disgust for God and anything resembling spiritual truth. Our natural response is to whip 'em into shape, to apply intense discipline so they will turn from scoffing and begin to think wisely. More than likely, however, confronting a scoffer is wasted effort, as Solomon reminded us:

> He who corrects a scoffer gets dishonor for himself,
> And he who reproves a wicked man gets insults for himself.
> Do not reprove a scoffer, or he will hate you,
> Reprove a wise man and he will love you. (9:7–8)

This passage explains why all these fall under the general heading of "the opposition." The scoffer won't listen to words of correction. He vigorously opposes it, not because he doesn't believe in God—he undoubtedly does. He scoffs because he refuses to acknowledge God's sovereignty. This character trait rejects all submission to any authority, and affects every relationship he has.

> A wise son accepts his father's discipline,
> But a scoffer does not listen to rebuke. (13:1)

> Drive out the scoffer, and contention will go out,
> Even strife and dishonor will cease. (22:10)

The devising of folly is sin,
And the scoffer is an abomination to men. (24:9)

Reflections

Do you know a scoffer, someone who mocks God, denigrates His people, and rejects spiritual truth? What has been your response in the past? How did this affect the scoffer and your relationship with him or her? How do these proverbs impact your response to him or her in the future?

Day 5: *Proverbs 1*
Intelligent Fools

Before we close this week's study, let's revisit the sages' fool. The English language defines a fool as someone who's a little mischievous or who makes foolish decisions. Hebrew culture, however, took the term *fool* far more seriously. We have considered three different kinds of internal opposition to divine leading, opposition that the Hebrew language describes using no less than four terms. Each term quantifies the level of foolishness in a person, and each successive term on the list reflects greater opposition than the previous one:

Peti: Undiscerning, unable, or unwilling to distinguish between truth and falsehood

Kasal: Lacking knowledge or practical experience; mentally sluggish

Nabal: Willfully closed to wisdom and brutishly destructive to self and others

Letz: Incorrigibly and willfully rebellious against God

You may notice that moral culpability increases with intellectual capacity. In other words, those who possessed the least intelligence were the least to blame for their opposition. For the Hebrews, the greatest fool of all was the opposer who possessed the greatest mental capacity. Solomon and the wise men of Israel didn't measure wisdom and foolishness in terms of IQ; for them, prudence is a measure of one's obedience to God.

Reflections

Take a few moments for some honest self-examination. Which kind of opposition do you struggle with the most? Do you see this same kind of opposition in others around you? How can you counteract these tendencies? In what ways can you involve wise people in helping you overcome your internal opposition to God's leading?

THE GRIND OF ADDICTION

Wine is a mocker, strong drink a brawler,
And whoever is intoxicated by it is not wise.

(Proverbs 20:1)

Who has woe? Who has sorrow?
Who has contentions? Who has complaining?
Who has wounds without cause?
Who has redness of eyes?
Those who linger long over wine,
Those who go to taste mixed wine.
Do not look on the wine when it is red,
When it sparkles in the cup,
When it goes down smoothly;
At the last it bites like a serpent
And stings like a viper.
Your eyes will see strange things
And your mind will utter perverse things.
And you will be like one who lies down in the middle of the
sea,
Or like one who lies down on the top of a mast.
"They struck me, but I did not become ill;
They beat me, but I did not know it.
When shall I awake?
I will seek another drink."

(23:29–35)

Day 1: *Proverbs 20, 23*
Timely Wisdom

I smile inside every time I hear someone say the Bible is irrelevant. Right away, I know that person is not at all acquainted with the pages of God's Book. As one who has been an expositor of Scripture for more than five decades, I am still occasionally stunned at how up-to-date and on-target the Bible really is.

As a good example of the relevance of Scripture, consider the daily grind of addiction. For many today, the physical and emotional dependence upon a particular substance is a grim, unrelenting reality, and statistics suggest that substance abuse isn't going away. If anything, the problem has expanded to include more people than ever. Long ago, alcohol and drug addiction left skid row to prey upon children in school yards. No longer is addiction the disease of the economic and cultural fringe; it is now a middle-class-family epidemic. Is there, then, any subject of greater relevance than this one?

Centuries ago, when the Lord directed His messengers to record His truth, this was a subject He chose not to overlook. So now, here we sit in the twenty-first century, surrounded by modern conveniences and unprecedented technology, yet the ancient sayings of a long-ago writer speak with fresh relevance.

This collection of wise sayings includes pertinent words and warnings for all who may be held captive by the effects of alcohol or the allure of other mind-altering substances. Chemical abuse is no longer hiding, whispered about by a select body of professionals behind closed doors; it is now out of the closet. All across the country groups gather in communities, colleges, and churches, not to scold or scream, preach or moralize, but to offer support. Trained professionals and recovering addicts take time to encourage, support, guide, and train one another. Most of them have been through the hellish nightmare of addiction themselves, so they understand what it feels like to be trapped, held captive by a bottle, a pill, a snort, an injection.

Reflections

Almost everyone has either struggled with substance abuse or knows someone who battles addiction. In what ways has this issue affected you personally? To what or whom do you turn for guidance and support?

Day 2: *Proverbs 20, 23*

Moderation versus Addiction

As we stated yesterday, substance abuse isn't limited to sleazy back alleys; you can find addiction almost anywhere. The penthouse suite owned by the high roller, nice homes where small children play, efficient offices where business is regularly transacted, military barracks where boredom reigns, professional sports teams where competition is fierce and money is plentiful—the problem knows no economic or social boundaries. This, however, isn't a recent phenomenon. Centuries ago, Solomon spoke to the issue. Despite his privileged position among the politically powerful and intellectually gifted, his writings reflect firsthand exposure. Solomon apparently either suffered addiction personally at some level, or he witnessed the condition in those close to him.

He personified alcohol as an abusive thug:

Wine is a mocker, strong drink a brawler,
And whoever is intoxicated by it is not wise. (20:1)

While at first Solomon appeared to target the substance, a closer look shows that he, in fact, took aim at addiction. Neither wine nor strong drink is inherently evil. In fact, wine was a necessary part of daily life in ancient times. This fermented grape juice contained alcohol, which kills harmful bacteria. Poured over a wound, it prevented infection. Mixed with water, it destroyed parasites. Consumed with a meal, it reduced the likelihood of food poisoning. For these reasons, Paul urged Timothy to consume wine in moderation for the sake of his health (1 Timothy 5:23). Up until the 1800s, when municipal water supplies first became safe to drink, everyone in the family—children included—drank wine . . . *in moderation.* Responsibly!

"Strong drink," however, was different. Also called "sweet wine," this beverage contained substantially more alcohol than what many cultures called "table wine." The makers of strong drink learned that mixing grapes with dried dates or pomegranates before fermentation yielded a drink that packs a bigger mind-altering punch. The same process worked for brewing strong beer, fermented from barley and then mixed with high-sugar fruit to produce higher alcohol content.

The key term in this proverb is the Hebrew word rendered "intoxicated," which may not be the best translation. The original verb means "to go astray, to err, to fail." The primary emphasis is to sin inadvertently, either through ignorance or by accident. In this context, wine and strong drink seduce their victim as a harlot entices a lover (Proverbs 5:20, 23). Moreover, this proverb implies that the sin is not merely one instance of drunkenness, but a downward direction in lifestyle. "Wine" and "strong drink" stand for addiction or compulsion. Therefore, the intoxication may not be merely the effects of alcohol on the brain but the influence of addiction on one's life.

Reflections

What is your attitude toward alcohol? What do you think shaped your perspective on the issue? What experience do you have with alcoholism and what impact has that had on your life? How is addiction like a seductive harlot?

Day 3: *Proverbs 20, 23*
A Deadly Substitute

Yesterday we discussed wine and strong drink. The chief concern of Solomon and the wise men was not the substance we call alcohol, but *addiction* to alcohol or the compulsion to drink it. The same concern exists for any other substance on which someone becomes dependent. Mind-altering drugs, of course, create similar problems, only quicker and more intensely. They cause "drunkenness" almost immediately, and many of these powerful chemicals cause physical addiction with just one use. For many years, illegal drugs claimed thousands of new addicts each year; now, prescription drugs pose an even greater problem.

While I certainly don't advocate the "responsible use" of cocaine or heroin—physicians declare there is no such thing—we must accept that addiction isn't driven by any particular substance; the problem doesn't lie outside the addict. The source of addiction is actually within the addict. Take one drug away from an addict, and that person will find another to replace it. Remove alcohol from the home of an alcoholic and she'll find another source. Addicts crave something they lack within. Note how Solomon depicted this craving in the lines of his poetic proverb.

> Who has woe? Who has sorrow?
> Who has contentions? Who has complaining?
> Who has wounds without cause?
> Who has redness of eyes?
> Those who linger long over wine,
> Those who go to taste mixed wine.
> Do not look on the wine when it is red,
> When it sparkles in the cup,
> When it goes down smoothly;
> At the last it bites like a serpent
> And stings like a viper. (23:29–32)

These first four lines describe the internal pain experienced by everyone but no one more so than the addict. While everyone has sorrows, interpersonal conflicts, issues prompting complaints, and deep emotional wounds, these are intensified by an addiction. Addicts look for comfort in a substance, but they find only temporary distraction followed by unpleasant physical consequences. The "redness of eyes" refers not only to crying but to the telltale bloodshot appearance of a person suffering from a hangover.

Healthy people suffer sorrows, contentions, struggles, and wounds without seeking alcohol or drugs, but addicts crave the distraction a substance offers. Note how addicts linger over wine and "mixed wine." They obsess over the appearance of the drink, becoming lost in the physical experience. Instead of finding relief from problems, addicts suffer ever deepening pain and sorrow. The "bite" of the serpent isn't merely a poisonous strike; the expression depicts a snake paralyzing its prey before consuming it whole.

Reflections

People who are prone to addictions have in common several personality traits. Do any of these describe you or someone close to you?

- Impulsive behavior and/or difficulty delaying gratification
- Poor balance in life, an all-or-nothing thinking
- Low tolerance for emotional pain
- Family history of addiction

These traits alone do not make a person an addict; they do, however, suggest he or she should remain aware of emotional pain and any activity that could become a compulsive escape.

Day 4: *Proverbs 20, 23*

Addiction's Downward Spiral

The problem of addiction goes beyond the abuse of alcohol or drugs. Addictions can develop out of virtually any substance or compulsive behavior. Very often people turn to certain behaviors because they find temporary relief from emotional pain. For example, a woman might soothe her troubled mind or cheer her depressed spirit with a shopping spree. The thrill of the deal and the enjoyment of having new things help her feel better . . . for a while. Studies have shown that compulsive behaviors actually trigger the release of chemicals that do bathe the brain in pleasant emotions. The effect is similar to that of an addictive substance, though less intense. Nevertheless, the experience sparked by these hormones and enzymes can become addictive and the withdrawal symptoms remarkably severe.

So the woman's shopping spree can make her feel better for a short while . . . until, of course, the bills come due. Then the consequences hit, triggering more stress and depression. The feelings of guilt, shame, stress, and depression then trigger a craving for the compulsive behavior or addictive substances—including food—and the downward cycle continues. The substance or behavior can be called addictive when at least three of the following seven signs appear:

1. The person develops a tolerance to the substance or activity such that increased amounts are necessary to achieve the desired effect.
2. The person suffers symptoms of withdrawal.
3. The person indulges in the substance or behavior to a greater degree or over a longer period than intended.
4. The person experiences persistent craving for the substance or activity and feels powerless to curtail or quit.
5. The person spends a great deal of time pursuing, obtaining, using, or recovering from the substance or activity.
6. The person sacrifices important social, occupational, personal, or recreational activities in order to use the substance or engage in the compulsive activity.
7. The addictive or compulsive behavior continues despite the experience of repeated and ongoing negative consequences.

If three or more of these signs become evident in someone's life, that person can experience a kind of mental transformation. Perceptions change. Defenses go up. Hypocrisy takes over. Note Solomon's depiction:

> Your eyes will see strange things
> And your mind will utter perverse things.
> And you will be like one who lies down in the middle of the sea,
> Or like one who lies down on the top of a mast. (23:33–34)

In these verses, the wise man described the feeling of drunkenness, including the hallucinations, skewed perspective, foolish decisions, and nausea. In a much deeper sense, however, Solomon described the mind of an addict under the deluding control of addiction. The king continued by speaking in the voice of the addict.

> They struck me, but I did not become ill;
> They beat me, but I did not know it.
> When shall I awake?
> I will seek another drink. (23:35)

Such negative consequences have little impact on the addict's decision about whether or not to continue destructive behavior. As soon as addicts are clear of the last round of difficulties—the last hangover, the last scrape with the law, the last blown relationship, the last job lost—they're planning the next opportunity to indulge their craving.

Review the seven signs of addiction. What, if anything, do these signs suggest about your behavior? To what or whom do you turn when you need comfort? Would people you respect affirm this emotional refuge?

Day 5: *Proverbs 20, 23*

Hope for the Hopeless

I am not foolish enough to suggest that within a week's time anyone could be free of an addiction or compulsion. While a few people tell of overnight transformations, these are the exception, not the norm. Still, let me assure you that, within just a week, you can be moving in a new, healthy direction. No addiction—I repeat: *no* addiction—is stronger than the Almighty. Never forget that His power stills storms and heals diseases and raises the dead. The wrong desires that come into your life aren't anything new and different.

> *Many others have faced exactly the same problems before you. And no temptation is irresistible. You can trust God to keep the temptation from becoming so strong that you can't stand up against it, for he has promised this and will do what he says. He will show you how to escape temptation's power so that you can bear up patiently against it. (1 Corinthians 10:13 TLB)*

The power of God notwithstanding, the grind of addiction is not easily overcome. While God may preserve you from your addiction, it's far more likely He intends to preserve you *through* your addiction. In other words, your healing will most likely be a long process. That's why many churches offer help in the form of ministries to addicts and their families. The stories of recovery that emerge from the ranks of those courageous folks are nothing short of thrilling.

I recall one account that involved a married couple with several small children. Both parents were addicted to cocaine, and it was not unusual for them to be high on the drug for a day or two each weekend. Thanks to the compassionate, gentle, yet firm determination of a few caring friends in one of these ministries, this couple found ways to "escape temptation's power." If some addiction has become your daily grind, I urge you to face it head-on. Contact your church or go online to see if a group addressing your particular addiction meets in your area.

Bottom line: Don't go it alone. If you struggle with an addiction or compulsion, you need the support and the accountability of a community to help guide you. You might need more intensive assistance through one-on-one therapy or maybe even an inpatient facility. Regardless, God has provided a way for you to escape this awful grind. Take that first step toward healing. Don't delay.

Reflections

Does your church provide assistance for people struggling with addictions? Most do not simply because they don't have sufficient numbers or funding. The pastor and leadership should, however, know where to direct people suffering from this affliction. Perhaps you could volunteer to help research alternative programs and establish partnerships with ministry leaders.

THE GRIND OF REVENGE

Do not rejoice when your enemy falls,
And do not let your heart be glad when he stumbles;
Or the LORD will see it and be displeased,
And turn His anger away from him.
Do not fret because of evildoers
Or be envious of the wicked;
For there will be no future for the evil man;
The lamp of the wicked will be put out.

(Proverbs 24:17–20)

If your enemy is hungry, give him food to eat;
And if he is thirsty, give him water to drink;
For you will heap burning coals on his head,
And the LORD will reward you.

(25:21–22)

Day 1: *Proverbs 24-25*
Poison to the Soul

I think Sir Francis Bacon had the right idea when he wrote, "Revenge is a kind of wild justice; which the more man's nature runs to, the more ought law to weed it out. . . . Certainly, in taking revenge a man is but even with his enemy; but in passing over it, he is superior, for it is a prince's part to pardon."[12] If you have spent much time around someone who is eaten up with the desire for revenge, someone nursing an attitude of resentment, you know how tragic a thing it is. These folks are walking containers of poison. That's because resentment never resolves itself; resentment corrodes anything it touches, breaks containment, and eventually kills its host. And to make things worse, innocent bystanders become victims of collateral damage when the pressure builds beyond control and suddenly explodes.

Take note of the first two lines in the preceding verses. They hold a clue as to the origins of resentment:

Do not rejoice when your enemy falls,
And do not let your heart be glad when he stumbles. (24:17)

The term rendered "enemy" means, literally, "hater" or "one who hates." This person has either harmed you in the past and has not repented or continues to take every opportunity to harm you now. Obviously, the proverb counsels against delighting in that person's downfall even though the temptation is great to see such misfortune as poetic justice. That desire, however, reveals a heart of bitterness and resentment that would take its own revenge if given the chance.

The next proverb explains why we must release this resentment and avoid taking pleasure in the pain of one who caused us harm:

Or the LORD will see [our attitude] and be displeased,
And turn His anger away from him. (24:18)

---

12 Francis Bacon, "Of Revenge," *The Essays, or Counsels, Civil and Moral of Francis Bacon*, ed. Samuel Harvey Reynolds (Oxford: Clarendon Press, 1890), 34.

When we fail to release our grip on resentment, we usurp God's role as the Supreme Judge of all people. By delighting in the downfall of our enemy, we accept that calamity as justice, and the focus of God's anger shifts away from the one who sinned against us and instead shines on our own sinful attitude. In that moment, we lose the moral high ground.

It's possible that revenge is your own personal daily grind. If so, trust me: you have a lot of company in that struggle. It is an ailment common to the majority of humanity. There isn't a culture in which revenge hasn't left its scars—but that doesn't excuse it! This is the week to expose revenge in all its ugliness. Like a poison that will eventually turn a healthy person into a walking corpse if it is ignored, this toxin must be neutralized or disposed of . . . the sooner, the better.

Reflections

Make a list of some people who have harmed you in some way and whom, in the quietness of your heart, you wish would suffer misfortune as payment for their sins against you. Keep this list private, of course, but we will refer to it throughout this week.

Day 2: *Proverbs 24-25*

Surrender Your Rights

If we accept that resentment is poisonous to the soul and that God demands we dispose of it, the next question is obvious: How? How can we rid ourselves of this toxic attitude? Here's where God's Word comes to our rescue. First, we must do something within ourselves that is painful. We must surrender our right to pursue our own justice. This is the first of two steps in forgiving someone. We will examine the second step tomorrow.

Leave Justice to God

There is a good reason we love justice. Fairness is a quality of God that we carry within us that, in part, bears His image. God is just. God is fair-minded. God believes in rewarding good behavior and allowing evildoers to suffer the punishment for their deeds. Nowhere in Scripture is the concept of justice declared bad. Neither will you find any condemnation for those who desire justice. Even so, God calls us to entrust Him with all matters requiring justice and to surrender our right to obtain it ourselves. God declared this early in the history of Israel:

> "Vengeance is Mine, and retribution,
> In due time their foot will slip;
> For the day of their calamity is near,
> And the impending things are hastening upon them."
> For the LORD will vindicate His people,
> And will have compassion on His servants.
> (Deuteronomy 32:35–36)

The proverb reassures us, "Do not fret because of evildoers or be envious of the wicked; for there will be no future for the evil man; the lamp of the wicked will be put out" (Proverbs 24:19–20). God gives us His solemn assurance that He will handle justice on our behalf and fulfill His role as Judge with absolute integrity. This promise frees us to leave past hurts in the past and to focus on making good decisions for the sake of creating a good future. When we do so, Paul the apostle stated, we "leave room for the wrath of God" (Romans 12:19) to accomplish its work. Read his counsel slowly and carefully:

Never pay back evil for evil to anyone. Respect what is right in the sight of all men. If possible, so far as it depends on you, be at peace with all men. Never take your own revenge, beloved, but leave room for the wrath of God, for it is written, "Vengeance is Mine, I will repay," says the Lord. (Romans 12:17–19)

Reflections

The first of two steps toward forgiving someone is surrendering your right to see justice done for the harm done to you. For each person on your list of offenders, repeat this prayer and mark the date.

> Lord, today, I officially hand over to You my right to see justice done concerning _____ and what this person did to harm me. I will neither seek retribution nor delight in his or her misfortunes. Justice is Your responsibility. Amen.

Don't rush the process. You may need several days before you can pray this sincerely for each person on your list. Work through the list, name by name, and genuinely relinquish your right to see justice done.

Day 3: *Proverbs 24–25*

Embrace Mercy

Yesterday we discovered that forgiving someone begins with your decision to surrender all rights to see justice done for the harm you suffered. It's not an easy decision. Letting someone off your moral hook takes great wisdom, courage, and faith. You aren't simply letting the matter drop; you are handing this person and your suffering over to God, trusting Him to do what is right. While this is extremely difficult to do, I have unsettling news for you. It's easy compared to the next step of genuine forgiveness.

Step 1: Leave justice to God. Now for step 2 . . .

Leave Mercy to God

Let me explain what I mean by way of a true story.

A man suffered the tragic loss of his wife to the advances of another man. Both men worked for the same Christian ministry, but through a bizarre twist of administrative blunders, the ministry was unable to fire the adulterous man—and he refused to quit. (The organization has since closed that gap in its policies!) The upright man could not afford to resign, and he struggled to find work elsewhere. Meanwhile, the two had to work in close proximity with one another for several weeks.

To his credit, the upright man turned the matter of justice over to God and clung to the words of Deuteronomy 32:35–36, a passage that begins, "Vengeance is Mine, and retribution." In fact, this man delighted in the notion that God would exact justice, and he longed for the day his enemy experienced divine vengeance and holy retribution. But as the days dragged on and the weeks rolled along, nothing happened. No fire. No brimstone. No heavenly payback fell upon the adulterous man.

Eventually, the upright man had to face an uncomfortable truth: God might, in fact, choose to show mercy to his adulterous enemy. What then? It's one thing to entrust God with vengeance in hopes of seeing justice done in due course, but it's quite another to affirm

God's decision to withhold retribution in a grand display of heavenly mercy!

But when the upright man was able to say, "Yes, Lord, vengeance is Yours . . . *and so is mercy*," he found peace. He had truly forgiven his adulterous enemy when he came to the point of trusting God to give either justice or mercy at His own discretion.

When you have accomplished both steps—"Leave justice to God" *and* "Leave mercy to God"—you are ready to not only give but also receive grace. That's our subject for tomorrow.

Reflections

Yesterday we looked at the first step in forgiving our enemies: we surrender our right to see justice enacted. Today, for each person on your list, repeat this prayer:

> Lord, today, I also affirm Your right to grant undeserved mercy to _____, who caused me great harm. I humbly submit to Your sovereign right to grant mercy as You see fit. Amen.

Day 4: *Proverbs 24–25*

Free-Flowing Grace

In a piece titled "Forgiveness Is a Condition for Our Own Freedom," Neil Anderson wrote the following:

> Forgiveness is not forgetting. People who try to forget find that they cannot. God says He will "remember no more" our sins (Hebrews 10:17), but God, being omniscient, cannot

forget. "Remember no more" means that God will never use the past against us (Psalm 103:12). Forgetting may be a result of forgiveness, but it is never the means of forgiveness. When we bring up the past against others, we haven't forgiven them.

Forgiveness is a choice, a crisis of the will. Since God requires us to forgive, it is something we can do. (He would never require us to do something we cannot do.)

Forgiveness is agreeing to live with the consequences of another person's sin. Forgiveness is costly; we pay the price of the evil we forgive. Yet you're going to live with those consequences whether you want to or not; your only choice is whether you will do so in the bitterness of unforgiveness or the freedom of forgiveness.[13]

When you have forgiven—when you have sincerely decided to surrender your right to see justice done and resolved never to hold the offense against your enemy—you have opened the way to extend grace toward the person who harmed you. While forgiveness removes the poison of resentment from your body, grace completely neutralizes the toxin so that no one can ever be harmed by it again.

Show Kindness to Your Enemy

Grace is simply kindness extended to another person regardless of merit—or the lack of it. Grace is showing kindness without first considering whether that person deserves it. Solomon and the wise men urge us,

If your enemy is hungry, give him food to eat;
And if he is thirsty, give him water to drink. (25:21)

---

13 Neil T. Anderson, *The Bondage Breaker* (Eugene, OR: Harvest House Publishers, 1990), 194–197.

In the Ancient Near-East, it was customary to extend hospitality to travelers, to friends and strangers alike. God, however, called His people to extend the same courtesy to enemies, to those who have harmed you without repenting and/or would take every opportunity to harm you again. God is not asking us to be fools; you need to protect yourself from further harm. Still, be kind. Give grace. In the words of Jesus, "Love your enemies, do good to those who hate you, bless those who curse you, pray for those who mistreat you" (Luke 6:27–28).

The following proverb suggests a potential result of extending unmerited kindness to our enemy, which is expressed in a curious figure of speech.

For you will heap burning coals on his head,
And the LORD will reward you. (25:22)

No one knows for certain the origin of this odd and ancient metaphor. Some suggest it points to an ancient Egyptian practice of carrying a pan of coals on one's head as a sign of contrition. I believe the phrase is merely an idiom describing humility, not unlike our expression "He came to me with his hat in his hand." In ancient times, allowing one's household fire to go out was seen as the epitome of irresponsibility. The humiliating experience of walking home from a neighbor's house with a pan of coals probably gave rise to this word picture for humility.

In my own experience, I have seen grace melt the hardest hearts and turn enemies into friends. It doesn't always work, but nothing can rival unmerited kindness for its ability to disarm our enemies. Hopefully our good conduct and our humility will bring about humility and repentance in return.

Reflections

For each person on your list, think of some way you can show kindness. Be wise, however. Don't give with any agenda and be sure to avoid embarrassing or shaming your now-forgiven enemy. In fact, start out with kind acts done anonymously.

Day 5: *Proverbs 24-25*

Our Great Challenge

Returning good for evil is not a complicated concept; it's very simple. Yet it is rare. It's one of the most difficult tasks we ever undertake in life. Let's be honest. Forgiving an offense is much easier when the guilty person is contrite and has sincerely apologized. But when the offender takes delight in our suffering or personally benefits from our downfall, choosing to treat him or her kindly defies everything we know about justice and fair play. Kindness is a response beyond our natural capability. It will require supernatural strength—and that is precisely what God has promised.

Embrace Grace

The apostle Paul's statement—"Do not be overcome by evil, but overcome evil with good" (Romans 12:21)—could be considered a mission statement for God's redemption of creation. His ultimate purpose in the world is to rescue the world from evil's grip, supernaturally transform the world, and then bring it back under the control of His righteousness. In other words, God will overcome the world's evil with His good. In following the command of Christ to "bless and do not curse" (Romans 12:14; Matthew 5:44) and by returning good for evil, we become "imitators of God" (Ephesians 5:1), as we become active participants in His work.

If, however, we refuse to join God in His work, if we reject His call to extend grace to our enemies as He does, the daily grind of revenge will continue to siphon our peace, drain our joy, and undermine our love until we do.

Reflections

Who presents the greatest challenge to your decision to forgive? What do you hope will happen if you withhold forgiveness? How realistic is this hope? What do you stand to gain by forgiving your enemies?

THE GRIND OF ENVY

Do not envy a man of violence
And do not choose any of his ways.
*For the devious are an abomination to the L*ORD*;*
But He is intimate with the upright.

(Proverbs 3:31–32)

For jealousy enrages a man,
And he will not spare in the day of vengeance.
He will not accept any ransom,
Nor will he be satisfied though you give many gifts.

(6:34–35)

A tranquil heart is life to the body,
But passion is rottenness to the bones.

(14:30)

Do not let your heart envy sinners,
*But live in the fear of the L*ORD *always.*
Surely there is a future,
And your hope will not be cut off.
Listen, my son, and be wise,
And direct your heart in the way.

(23:17–19)

Do not be envious of evil men,
Nor desire to be with them;

For their minds devise violence,
And their lips talk of trouble.

(24:1–2)

Do not fret because of evildoers
Or be envious of the wicked;
For there will be no future for the evil man;
The lamp of the wicked will be put out.

(24:19–20)

Wrath is fierce and anger is a flood,
But who can stand before jealousy?

(27:4)

Day 1: *Proverbs 3, 6, 14, 23-24, 27*

A Thief and a Tyrant

Petrarch hit the nail on the head when he wrote, "Five great enemies of peace inhabit within us: avarice, ambition, envy, anger, and pride; and if those enemies were to be banished, we should infallibly enjoy perpetual peace." Envy is definitely one of the great enemies of inner peace. Like a thief, it slides into the heart under cover of darkness and steals away contentment.

Envy is the desire to become better or at least equal to one's peers in achievement, excellence, or possessions. The ancients referred to envy as a malignant or hostile feeling. Augustine listed it among the passions that "rage like tyrants, and throw into confusion the whole soul and life of man with storms from every quarter."[14] He then described such a soul as having an "eagerness to win what was not possessed . . . Wherever he turns, avarice can confine him, self-indulgence dissipate him, ambition master him, pride puff him up, envy torture him, sloth drug him."[15]

Torture is an appropriate description of what envy does. This disease of the spirit exacts a heavy toll on its victims.

Jealousy and *envy* are often used interchangeably, but there is a small, yet profound difference between the two. Jealousy begins with full hands and then moves through life in the terror of losing something. It is fueled by the fear of loss, and it fuels an all-out, life-or-death struggle to maintain those possessions. Envy, however, begins with empty hands, lamenting what it does not have. In *Purgatorio*, Dante portrayed this character flaw as "a blind beggar whose eyelids are sewn shut." One who is envious suffers greatly because he is sewn up within himself.

Jealousy wants to preserve what it already has; envy wants to gain what another possesses.

Reflections

On a scale of one to ten, rate your level of contentment with your current level of wealth and possessions. What typically prompts your desire to have more? If you could maintain your present lifestyle in a third-world country, how do you think your attitude would change regarding material wealth?

---

14 Saint Augustine, *On Free Choice of the Will*, I.xi.22.
15 Ibid.

Day 2: *Proverbs 3, 6, 14, 23-24, 27*

The Ugly *Red* Monster

You may have heard the expression "green with envy" or envy referred to as "the green-eyed monster." In the Bible, however, envy had the Hebrews seeing red. The Hebrew word translated "envy" and "jealousy" is *quanah*, which means "to be intensely red." This word vividly pictures someone seething with red-faced anger as a surge of blood flushes one's skin, signaling a rush of fierce emotion. To demonstrate the grim irony of language, *zeal* and *ardor* and *envy* all come from a common linguistic root. The same emotion that "enrages a man" (Proverbs 6:34) also floods him with passionate zeal to defend his country or adore his wife and children.

The Bible most often uses *quanah* in the negative sense. Every instance in the book of Proverbs warns against coveting the wealth and possessions evil people gain through dishonest means: "Do not envy a man of violence" (3:31); "Do not let your heart envy sinners" (23:17); "Do not be envious of evil men, nor desire to be with them" (24:1); "Do not fret because of evildoers or be envious of the wicked" (24:19).

I find these warnings extremely significant, although this source of envy shouldn't surprise us. A favorite unguarded mind game so many folks play is to imagine how stimulating it would be to throw restraint to the winds, to live without the inconvenience of ethics, do anything, go anywhere, and let it all hang out. Let's face facts: sin has its sensual and seasonal pleasures. They may be short-lived and passing (Hebrews 11:25), but they're certainly not dull and boring!

English and Hebrew assign different colors to the monster called "envy," but they acknowledge the same ultimate outcome of this destructive emotion. Envy leads to sin (Proverbs 14:30), and sin leads to shame, an emotion represented by the color red. When the Russians were caught spying in England, Margaret Thatcher said, "They were caught red-handed, and now they are red-faced." So it is with those who indulge the temptation of envy.

So, beware the green of envy. It will eventually have everyone seeing red.

Reflections

What keeps you living within the moral and ethical boundaries established by the Scriptures? What prevents you from becoming envious of those who do not accept or obey biblical guidelines?

Day 3: Proverbs 3, 6, 14, 23-24, 27
The Destructive Potential of Envy

Let's be honest. Sometimes sin seems to have more to offer us than righteousness does. If we observe the world today, the wicked appear to have all the advantages. Haven't you noticed? They maneuver their way through life with relative ease, they get out of trouble by lying and cheating, they can own and drive whatever, live wherever, and con whomever they wish to get whatever they want. And it seems as though they usually get away with it, somehow escaping all accountability and responsibility. If something gets to be a hassle, bail out of it! If somebody gets in the way, walk over him or her! When we compare that self-satisfying lifestyle to the disciplines of devotion to God and the restraints of His righteous standards, it doesn't take an advanced degree to understand how envy can creep in. And we don't only envy the ungodly. We can be just as envious of our fellow Christians.

And envy happens so quickly! And it can happen in dozens of life's scenes:

- When we hear a more polished speaker
- When we watch a more capable leader
- When we visit a bigger church
- When we read a better book
- When we meet a more beautiful woman or a more successful man
- When we listen to a more effective evangelist
- When we ride in a more luxurious car
- When we listen to a more popular singer

The envy list has no end. Not even preachers are immune! Perhaps this is your daily grind, and it may be intensifying as you see your age outpacing your accomplishments. There was once a time when you could push that feeling away and keep a lid on it. Hope kept its power diffused. But as you get older and your problems chip away at your patience, perhaps your faith is approaching a significant crisis.

Tomorrow, we will discover the remedy for the disease of envy. For now, however, think about the effects of envy on your spiritual life.

Reflections

What circumstances most often cause you to doubt your faith or question your godly manner of life? How do you respond to this crisis? What helps you get back on track?

Day 4: *Proverbs 3, 6, 14, 23–24, 27*

The Cure for the Common Envy

Asaph struggled with envy. He had a hard time making sense of the fact that righteous people could barely make ends meet while evil people enjoyed opulent, sumptuous lifestyles. This apparent injustice bothered him so much that his faith almost failed him. This crisis of belief might have gone unnoticed—who hasn't struggled with doubt?—were it not for the fact he was the leader of worship in Israel, responsible for arranging and conducting services for God's covenant people. But rather than hide his doubts, Asaph wrote a lengthy song, detailing the questions he pondered and retracing his halting steps through a maze of theological confusion.

At one point in Psalm 73, he stated flatly, "As for me, my feet came close to stumbling, my steps had almost slipped. For I was envious of the arrogant" (vv. 2–3). He goes on to detail the reasons for his envy. In short, the arrogant grew richer as the godly grew poorer. And, to make matters worse, the ungodly abused the godly and became scorners of God. As if Asaph's own poverty wasn't unsettling enough, it appeared to him that God had rewarded the wrong people for their wrong behavior. At the time, sin and rebellion seemed the more attractive way of life!

Asaph's crisis of faith found resolution, however, when he turned his eyes away from material wealth to worship God.

It was troublesome in my sight
Until I came into the sanctuary of God;
Then I perceived their end. (Psalm 73:16–17)

Refocusing his attention on God rather than his circumstances, Asaph overcame his envy. Worshiping the Lord reoriented his perspective in three specific ways:

First, Asaph rearranged his priorities: wisdom is more important than wealth.

Second, he regained an eternal perspective: the true rewards of faithfulness come later.

Third, he reassessed his values: intimacy with God is the greatest treasure of all.

Reflections

How often do you truly worship? In what ways can you incorporate worship into your weekly routine between Sundays? How can you become an encouragement and a support for others who struggle with doubt?

Day 5: Proverbs 3, 6, 14, 23-24, 27
The Great Physician

Envy is a disease of the soul you can ignore for a while, but eventually you must address it. Like a slow-growing cancer, envy will eventually consume you. As you grow older and encounter more of the injustices of life, you won't be able to enjoy the advantages you have because less deserving people appear to have privileges and possessions you do not. As time passes, this awareness of others' blessings will rob you of that "perpetual peace" as envy tortures you with its deceptive whisperings. What is worse, instead of your being happy for others whom God has blessed, you grow more suspicious or resentful, maybe downright angry. "Envy," reminds Solomon, "enrages a man."

This is the week to come to terms with envy. How much more peaceful to be contented with what God provides! How much better to "rejoice with those who rejoice"! A mark of maturity is the ability to appreciate another more gifted than we . . . to applaud another more honored than we . . . to enjoy another more blessed than we. Such a wholesome response underscores our confidence in and allegiance to the sovereignty of God, who "puts down one and exalts another" (Psalm 75:7).

I urge you to join Solomon, the wise men of Israel, and Asaph: expose your inner struggle with envy to the Physician of your soul. Like revenge, envy is a malignancy we dare not ignore. Let's invite the Physician to use His scalpel to dig deeply to excise the malignancy. If ignored, envy can become a terminal illness of your soul. Invite God to cut it out today!

Reflections

You know the dangers of envy, and we have discovered the cure. Still, the human heart enjoys the short-term pleasures of envy. Why do you think we find envy so appealing? What long-term effect might envy have on a person's spiritual life? In what ways can other people help you overcome envy in your own life?

THE GRIND OF INTOLERANCE

A man's discretion makes him slow to anger,
And it is his glory to overlook a transgression.

(Proverbs 19:11)

Deliver those who are being taken away to death,
And those who are staggering to slaughter, Oh hold them
back.
If you say, "See, we did not know this,"
Does He not consider it who weighs the hearts?
And does He not know it who keeps your soul?
And will He not render to man according to his work?

(24:11–12)

To show partiality is not good,
Because for a piece of bread a man will transgress.

(28:21)

The righteous is concerned for the rights of the poor,
The wicked does not understand such concern.

(29:7)

There is a kind of man who curses his father
And does not bless his mother.
There is a kind who is pure in his own eyes,
Yet is not washed from his filthiness.
There is a kind—oh how lofty are his eyes!

And his eyelids are raised in arrogance.
There is a kind of man whose teeth are like swords
And his jaw teeth like knives,
To devour the afflicted from the earth
And the needy from among men.

(30:11–14)

Day I: *Proverbs 19, 24, 28–30*

Tolerance at Its Best

In the past several years, *tolerance* has become a dirty word among conservative evangelicals. That's unfortunate, although I can see why the concept has become so controversial. Perhaps our examination of intolerance should begin with a proper definition of *tolerance*. Let's clarify what we mean and—more importantly— what we *do not* mean by *tolerance*.

In the best Christian sense of the term, tolerance is an important aspect of grace. Tolerance provides "wobble room" for those who struggle to measure up. Tolerance allows growing room for young and restless children. It smiles at rather than frowns on the struggling new believer. Instead of rigidly pointing to the rules and rehearsing the failures of the fallen, tolerance stoops to help the fallen and reaches out to offer fresh hope and enduring acceptance. In my book *The Grace Awakening*, I called tolerance "the grace to let others be," which I further explained this way:[16]

---

16 Charles R. Swindoll, *The Grace Awakening* (Nashville: W Publishing Group, 2003), 147–155.

1. Accepting others is basic to letting them be.
2. Refusing to dictate to others allows the Lord freedom to direct their lives.
3. Freeing others means we never assume a position we're not qualified to fill.
4. Loving others requires us to express our liberty wisely.

Intolerance is the antithesis of all that I have just described. It is an unwillingness to "overlook a transgression" (Proverbs 19:11); it tightens the strings of guilt and verbalizes a lot of shoulds and musts. The heart of the intolerant—their heart of stone—remains unbreakable, impenetrable, judgmental, and without compassion.

This lack of tolerance is not overt, but subtle. You may detect it in a look; it is not usually spoken. To draw upon Solomon's saying, instead of delivering those who are going under, those "staggering to slaughter," the intolerant excuse their failure to help by saying, "We did not know this" (24:11–12). But the Lord knows better. The Lord is well aware of even the slightest spirit of partiality hidden in our hearts.

Reflections

Intolerance is a daily grind on everyone, both victims and perpetrators. How have you experienced intolerance? What impact did it have on your desire and ability to live? How has your intolerance made life more difficult for someone? How can you make that right?

Day 2: *Proverbs 19, 24, 28-30*

The Dark Side of Tolerance

The founders of the United States formed this nation on the premise that each individual will one day stand before God and give an answer for his or her beliefs and conduct. The US was in fact the first modern state to establish an official policy of religious tolerance, which it formalized in the first amendment to the Constitution:

> Congress shall make no law respecting an establishment of religion, or prohibiting the free exercise thereof; or abridging the freedom of speech, or of the press; or the right of the people peaceably to assemble, and to petition the Government for a redress of grievances.

In forty-five words, the founders of America granted all citizens "the grace to let others be." The Constitution protects us from governmental interference as well as from our neighbors' intrusion on our relationship with God. This is political legislation and religious tolerance at its best. This policy allows people who disagree to live in reasonable harmony with one another.

In recent years, however, the term *tolerance* has taken a disturbing turn. As a buzzword of political correctness, it now means we must not only live peaceably with those who hold rival beliefs, but we must also accept their beliefs as being equally as true as our own! By extension, if we do not affirm the conduct or beliefs of others, we are guilty of intolerance. Consider, for example, a group of people deciding that polygamy is a valid alternative lifestyle, and they lobby the government to legally recognize and affirm multiple marriages. People who exercise their first-amendment right to disagree openly then become guilty of "intolerance." Consequently, *tolerance* has sadly become a negative term among many faithful believers in Christ.

Clearly, this is not the kind of tolerance affirmed by the Scriptures. As we discuss the issues of tolerance and intolerance, bear in mind that no genuine believer can affirm anything contrary to the Bible as good or true.

Reflections

In what ways have you been impacted by the improper definition of *tolerance* and *intolerance*? How did you respond? Having a better definition of these terms, how will you respond to future accusations that you are intolerant?

Day 3: *Proverbs 19, 24, 28-30*

The Wounds of Intolerance

Is intolerance one of your daily grinds? Be honest. Do you have difficulty leaving room for opinions you don't agree with or the conduct of those who fail to measure up? I can think of a number of ways intolerance rears its head:

- The healthy can be impatient with the sickly.
- The strong have trouble empathizing with the weak.
- The quick have little patience with the slow.
- The productive lack understanding for the drudge.
- The wealthy can scarcely imagine the pain of poverty.
- The quick minds know nothing of the embarrassment of being a slow learner.

- The coordinated shake their heads at the awkward.
- The pragmatic criticize the philosophical.
- The philosophical chide the pragmatists for their structure.
- The engineer has little appreciation for the artist.
- The stable and secure struggle to understand the fragile and fearful.

Karl Menninger wrote with keen perception,

When a trout rising to a fly gets hooked on a line and finds himself unable to swim about freely, he begins with a fight which results in struggles and splashes and sometimes an escape. Often, of course, the situation is too tough for him. In the same way the human being struggles with his environment and with the hooks that catch him. Sometimes he masters his difficulties; sometimes they are too much for him. His struggles are all that the world sees and it naturally misunderstands them. It is hard for a free fish to understand what is happening to a hooked one.[17]

Perhaps you are a "free fish." Having never felt the sting of a hook or the choking panic of being caught, you would do well to keep your pride in check!

Reflections

In what ways have other people misunderstood your personal struggles? How do your own struggles help you give grace to others? How do you respond to someone whose struggles you have never experienced? What can you do to offer them support?

---

17 Karl A. Menninger in Chaim Potok, *The Chosen* (frontispiece). (New York: Ballantine Books, 1967).

Day 4: *Proverbs 19, 24, 28-30*
Teeth Like Swords

This is an excellent time to bring out into the open even the slightest intolerance lurking in your life and place it before the Lord. The book of Proverbs offers a compelling reason to do so by painting a picture of someone we do not want to become.

There is a kind of man who curses his father
And does not bless his mother.
There is a kind who is pure in his own eyes,
Yet is not washed from his filthiness.
There is a kind—oh how lofty are his eyes!
And his eyelids are raised in arrogance.
There is a kind of man whose teeth are like swords
And his jaw teeth like knives,
To devour the afflicted from the earth
And the needy from among men. (Proverbs 30:11–14)

Take note of how the author described certain kinds of people who are "pure in their own eyes," whose "eyelids are raised in arrogance," yet who is "not washed from his filthiness." The hypocrite wears a mask of superiority to conceal his own sinfulness. The intolerant often begin to believe their own press, truly seeing themselves as morally superior despite the proliferation of sin in their lives. Interestingly, their teeth become swordlike, sharp as knives, and like a predatory beast they feed on less aggressive creatures.

Whom do they devour? "The afflicted . . . the needy" (v. 14). Why, of course! Like predators in the wild, the intolerant invariably choose to devour the weak, the small, the young, the wounded, the vulnerable. They target those they consider beneath them.

Reflections

Describe what you have seen about how the intolerant operate. What tactics do they employ to hide their own deeds and defects? Why do you think they prey on others? What can you do to support their victims? Are you guilty of intolerance?

Day 5: *Proverbs 19, 24, 28-30*
Generous with Grace

B efore closing off our study of intolerance, two more sayings are worth our attention:

The generous man will be prosperous,
And he who waters will himself be watered. (11:25)

The righteous is concerned for the rights of the poor,
The wicked does not understand such concern. (29:7)

The most obvious interpretation of the first proverb urges us to be generous with our money, but we would be wise to broaden the application to include being generous of spirit, to be broad shouldered and bighearted. Such individuals will be generous with grace, and the same will come back to them. Others, in turn, respond to grace with acceptance and tolerance.

The second proverb states that those who are truly righteous do not oppress the less fortunate. Instead, they become advocates, working to see that the less fortunate receive fair treatment. The term translated "rights" refers to evenhanded judgment, to unrestricted access to a court where an impartial judge can hear their case and then uphold the law. This kind of tolerance seeks justice and fairness for all. It does not excuse sin, but it also safeguards the guilty from overly harsh treatment.

Jesus serves as a worthy example of this. Our Lord knew no sin, did no sin, had no sin. He was never "hooked" by evil, yet His heart went out to those who had been and who were ashamed of their sin. On one occasion He even defended a woman caught in the very act of adultery. Having saved her from unjust treatment by a band of bloodthirsty hypocrites, Jesus said, "Go. From now on sin no more" (John 8:11).

This is the brand of tolerance God desires in His people. Remain firm on the standards of righteousness and be generous with grace toward those who struggle to measure up. After all, who among us has not failed? Who has not needed grace?

Reflections

Is there someone you know who could use an arm around a shoulder, a word of encouragement, or a few hours of companionship? Perhaps this person doesn't measure up to the expectations of others, holds a different opinion on a controversial subject, or recently endured a time of personal disappointment. Are you willing to risk contact? Can you set aside your own prejudices and become an advocate?

THE GRIND OF EXCUSE MAKING

Four things are small on the earth,
But they are exceedingly wise:
The ants are not a strong people,
But they prepare their food in the summer;
The shephanim are not mighty people,
Yet they make their houses in the rocks;
The locusts have no king,
Yet all of them go out in ranks;
The lizard you may grasp with the hands,
Yet it is in kings' palaces.

(Proverbs 30:24–28)

Day 1: *Proverbs 30*
Diligence

A nts, conies, locusts, lizards—sounds like a roll call for No-ah's ark or perhaps the cast of characters in an animated fea-ture film. Actually, these are four creatures discussed in Proverbs 30:24–28, each illustrating a quality wise people should possess. The opening statement declares, each of these four creatures is "small on the earth, but they are exceedingly wise" (v. 24). Each offers the reader an intriguing contrast: a noteworthy characteristic offsets a significant limitation. Naturally, these contrasts invite us to examine each creature and then appreciate how wisdom applied overcomes disadvantages.

The Ant

Sooner or later, everyone feels powerless or inadequate. That happened to me during my third year of seminary. By then, we had welcomed our first child, and I had become a pastoral assistant to my mentor, Dr. Dwight Pentecost, a position that allowed me to earn an adequate living. To those responsibilities, I added twenty-one credit hours and audited two other courses—not a good decision! Around that time, Cynthia's mother was dying of cancer, I passed two kidney stones, and a drunk driver slammed into our car, breaking our son's jaw and totaling the vehicle. To be honest, I felt like giving up. The demands on my time and energy stretched me to the breaking point. Medical expenses from the pregnancy and the accident rose like a mountain in front of me. Physically exhausted and spiritually drained, I was overcome with despair one particular evening. I stood behind our little dwelling under a giant Texas sky, staring into the starry expanse, feeling extremely tiny and inadequate, pouring out my heart to God.

Proverbs 30:25 states that the ants are not "strong." Unlike a great civilization of people, they are vulnerable to attack and easily destroyed. They thrive despite their lack of might because they don't quit. They serve their community without having taskmasters bark orders. They work each day to maintain a secure place to live. They dutifully gather food during times of plenty in order to survive inevitable difficulties. The ant provides a worthy example of how diligence, dedication, foresight, and industriousness—little by little, day by day—keep the colony fed, warmed, and protected.

On that difficult night, God reminded me that I wasn't responsible for anything except giving my very best to the day in front of me.

I couldn't see how we would pay our bills, complete seminary, and make a comfortable home for our child, but I could take on the next day with diligence. Then, day by day and little by little, we emerged from that difficult season.

Reflections

What challenges do you face that have you feeling overwhelmed? Begin by establishing a long-term plan for addressing the issue, perhaps with the help of appropriately trained professionals. Then focus only on the day in front of you and give it your very best.

Day 2: Proverbs 30
Prudence

As the great theologian and sage Clint Eastwood once said, "A man's got to know his limitations." Children enter the world with no concept of the word *can't*. Soon, however, the world begins to teach them that some things are, indeed, beyond their reach. By the time we reach adulthood, several defeats have helped delineate our capabilities. Unfortunately, these failures may steal our confidence so that we become timid, unwilling to try to achieve worthy and reachable goals. Wise people know their limitations, but they don't allow those limitations to become excuses.

The Cony

Agur, the wise man who wrote this set of proverbs, used an animal well known in Judea to illustrate an admirable characteristic of wisdom. The word rendered "badger" in many translations is actually *shaphan* in Hebrew. The plural form is *shephanim*. Unlike the fierce badger familiar to most people, the *shaphan* could be a rock cony or species of hyrax, a creature that resembles a large guinea pig with short ears, a chubby body, a stubby tail, and short, brown fur. Adults can grow to 20 inches (50 cm) in length and tip the scales at 9 pounds (4 kg). Like rabbits and prairie dogs, they are very docile animals.

They feed on vegetation in the morning and evening, live in burrows, and form tight-knit communities. *Shephanim* have no natural defenses against animals that would prey on them, animals like leopards, snakes, wolves, and eagles. Despite the fact that everything wants to eat them and they are hunted on the ground and from the sky, very few *shephanim* actually fall victim to their predators. That's because they live in very secure refuges, remain close to home, and have a remarkably complex sentry system. The older adults usually take positions on prominent lookout spots and sound the alarm at the first sign of danger.

Compared to many animals, the *shephanim* have it tough. They live in harsh terrain and are relatively defenseless creatures. Yet they thrive! They recognize their own limitations and make the most of their circumstances. Moreover, they use their greatest asset, their community, to the greatest advantage.

All of us have limitations, but at least one key to success in life is refusing to allow limitations to become excuses and finding a way to accomplish your goals regardless.

Reflections

What limitations threaten to keep you down? A physical disability? Financial woes? Social or political obstacles? While acknowledging your limitations, consider how you can improvise, adapt, and overcome in order to reach your goals. How can your community be part of the solution and help you reach your goals?

Day 3: *Proverbs 30*

Cooperation

Great civilizations often achieve great things because they have a great leader who casts a vision, marshals their resources, organizes their members, inspires their action, and of course, goes before them. People generally fare better when they have a leader, when someone helps them cooperate and accomplish what can only be achieved with a coordinated effort. But what if there is no leader?

The Locust

The Hebrew sage Agur penned just two lines about the locust, but those lines refer to a phenomenon that every citizen of Israel had personally witnessed. Agur referred to the locust, an insect very similar to the grasshopper, the primary difference being their tendency to swarm.

Farmers feared few things more than they feared a plague of locusts. Those insects can breed out of control, congregate, and then begin to move from field to field, consuming every crop they encounter. Each adult can eat its own weight in food. Multiply that one locust by the hundreds of thousands, give them crops to eat, and you have a first-rate, Old Testament pestilence on your hands. Some swarms sound like a commercial jetliner passing overhead.

According to the wise man, however, these creatures have no leader, no one to plan, organize, coordinate, and execute. Nevertheless, locusts become a strategically aligned team that "[goes] out in ranks" to wreak havoc on endless acres of crops, which they devour with terrifying efficiency. The word translated "ranks" usually refs to archers, who maintained a prescribed space between each man. The writer used this image to emphasize the presence of cooperation within the swarm.

The secret to the success of a locust swarm is cooperation. They could all fly off in a hundred different directions. Instead, they move together from place to place, flying in formation, as it were, feeding and breeding until they become an unstoppable force. They illustrate a principle that wise people do not neglect: what we cannot accomplish on our own, we can achieve together.

Reflections

Earlier you considered the challenges you face. Review them again and consider how you might join with others, work in concert with them, and solve your mutual problems together. For example, single mothers in need of child care might band together to either share the cost of hiring some help or schedule times to watch one another's children. Find people with similar challenges, get together, and brainstorm creative ideas of how to meet those challenges.

Day 4: *Proverbs 30*

Helpfulness

As we consider Agur's fourth and final animal illustration, we must wrestle with an unusually enigmatic proverb. We typically encounter this problem whenever a statement depends heavily upon a shared cultural experience that no longer exists. For example, the American expression "He came to me with his hat in his hand" depends heavily upon the shared experience of the Great Depression. During those desperate years, a cash-strapped man might have no other choice than to approach a group of friends for a donation. It was a humiliating experience for him to hold out his hat in the desperate hope they would drop a few precious coins into it. Very few people today know the meaning of this expression because they never witnessed this practice—and very few men even wear hats today! Anyway, at the risk of adding one more possible interpretation of Proverbs 30:28 to an already long list, I would suggest that the author intends to illustrate the wise virtue of being helpful.

The Lizard

The Hebrew word rendered "lizard" in most translations is *semamit*, a word that appears only this once in the Old Testament. Most experts believe it refers to a kind of gecko. A similar word in Arabic denotes a species of lizard, leading many to suggest it is a common house lizard that feeds on insects and other pests. While one can easily "grasp with the hands" a lizard and kill it, most people tolerated them—in fact, gave them the run of the house— because the creatures did little harm and actually helped to solve a problem.

The application should be relatively obvious. Being small and vulnerable, house lizards are welcome in every home, including the palaces of kings, because they cause no harm and, in fact, improve their environment. The same can be said of wise people. Despite any weaknesses, disabilities, or disadvantages, everyone can find a way to be helpful. Even cruel, selfish people will show favor to someone who causes them no harm and finds ways to be beneficial.

Reflections

For the next several weeks, look for ways to be helpful wherever you happen to be. At work, a friend's party, the shopping center, church—anywhere and everywhere you go, make a conscious effort to notice a need, regardless of how small or insignificant, and take the initiative to be helpful. Notice how your helpfulness affects the environment and the response you receive from others.

Day 5: *Proverbs 30*
Freedom in Truth

Ants, conies, locusts, and lizards offer very significant illustrations of virtues everyone can apply to their life. These four animals also demonstrate how to escape the daily grind of excuse making. These four diverse creatures share a common predicament: they are relatively small, fairly powerless, and easily destroyed. But these species continue to thrive because, for each, a particular virtue more than offsets their disadvantages: the ant is diligent; the cony is prudent; the locust is cooperative; and the lizard is helpful.

Let these interesting critters prompt you to take an unflinching look at challenges you face and perhaps at your tendency to avoid the hard questions, ignore the warnings of a friend, and deny criticism that could prove extremely beneficial. When you embrace your weaknesses or challenges rather than deny, ignore, or make excuses, you become wise. When you accept difficult truths, you have an opportunity to consider alternatives, to apply one of the four virtues that we examined this week—diligence, prudence, cooperation, and helpfulness—and to find a way to overcome your difficulties.

Using what you have learned this week, work hard at coming to terms with your disabilities—we all have them in some form or another—and avoid making excuses. Living beyond that daily grind starts when you embrace the truth. Then you have the opportunity to become wise.

Reflections

Take a few moments to again examine your weaknesses or the challenges you face. When in the past have you denied them, ignored them, or made excuses for them? If you embrace your shortcomings without shame or self-condemnation, how will that change your perspective on life for the better? How will this acceptance of reality affect your ability to make realistic plans?

THE GRIND OF FINANCIAL IRRESPONSIBILITY

Honor the LORD from your wealth
And from the first of all your produce;
So your barns will be filled with plenty
And your vats will overflow with new wine.

(Proverbs 3:9–10)

It is the blessing of the LORD that makes rich,
And He adds no sorrow to it.

(10:22)

How much better it is to get wisdom than gold!
And to get understanding is to be chosen above silver.

(16:16)

The rich rules over the poor,
And the borrower becomes the lender's slave.

(22:7)

Do not be among those who give pledges,
Among those who become guarantors for debts.
If you have nothing with which to pay,
Why should he take your bed from under you?

(22:26–27)

Do not weary yourself to gain wealth,
Cease from your consideration of it.

When you set your eyes on it, it is gone.
For wealth certainly makes itself wings
Like an eagle that flies toward the heavens.

(23:4–5)

He who tills his land will have plenty of food,
But he who follows empty pursuits will have poverty in
plenty.
A faithful man will abound with blessings,
But he who makes haste to be rich will not go unpunished.

(28:19–20)

A man with an evil eye hastens after wealth
And does not know that want will come upon him.

(28:22)

Day I: *Proverbs 3, 10, 16, 22, 23, 28*
Truth and Freedom

Few "grinds" in life are more nerve-racking and energy draining than those that result from financial irresponsibility. Many
are the headaches and heartaches of being overextended. Great
are the worries of those, for example, who continue to increase
their indebtedness, spend impulsively, or loan money to others
indiscriminately.

These words may sting your conscience if they describe your
situation. What's worse, they may describe where you have been off
and on for as long as you can remember. It may not bring much

comfort to know that you are not alone, but there is perhaps no more common problem among Americans than this one. So common is it that places of business must protect themselves from this phenomenon by operating under strict guidelines. All this reminds me of a sign that made me smile. It hangs in a Fort Lauderdale restaurant:

IF YOU ARE OVER 80 YEARS OLD AND ACCOMPANIED BY YOUR PARENTS, WE WILL CASH YOUR CHECK.

Another wag once described our economic times with these three definitions:

Recession: When the man next door loses his job
Depression: When you lose your job
Panic: When your wife loses her job

Many families today have reached the place where the wife's working outside the home isn't merely optional; it's a necessity.

To the surprise of no one, Scripture's statements about money are numerous. Long before Ben Franklin penned his wit and wisdom in *Poor Richard's Almanac*, Solomon's words offered wise counsel that was available for all to read. And when I attempted to categorize the teachings, I saw that Solomon's sayings cover a broad spectrum of subjects, including getting money (earning and inheriting), releasing money (spending, squandering, loaning, and giving), investing money, saving money, and handling money wisely. The economic terms used in Scripture are many: *money, wealth, riches, lending, borrowing, spending, giving, losing, silver, gold, plenty, abundance, want, poverty,* and a half dozen others.

Having traced the subject of finances throughout Solomon's sayings, I discovered six principles of money management. Over the next few days, we will examine each one and determine how to apply it to life today.

Reflections

In preparation for this week, get a bank statement for all of your accounts (checking, savings, credit cards, etc.). Set aside some time to examine them. Take note of spending patterns. Using colored pens, highlight items according to categories, such as household expenses (mortgage, rent, utilities); entertainment; education; giving; and discretionary spending. For some readers, this will be a difficult assignment. As you persevere, remember what Jesus said: truth leads to freedom (John 8:32).

Day 2: *Proverbs 3, 10, 16, 22, 23, 28*

Where Your Treasure Is

While studying the book of Proverbs, I discovered several principles that helped me understand money management from God's perspective. These aren't tax-saving tips or strategies for gaining wealth, although doing things God's way certainly can't hurt. The Lord is more concerned about how our handling of money affects our spiritual life and how our finances impact our relationship with Him and His people.

Here is the first principle:

1. Those who honor God with their money are blessed in return.

Honor the LORD from your wealth
And from the first of all your produce;
So your barns will be filled with plenty
And your vats will overflow with new wine. (Proverbs 3:9–10)

It is the blessing of the LORD that makes rich,
And He adds no sorrow to it. (10:22)

Adversity pursues sinners,
But the righteous will be rewarded with prosperity. (13:21)

I have said for years that you can tell much more about an individual's dedication to God by looking at that person's bank statement than by looking at his or her Bible. Again and again throughout Scripture, we read of the blessings God grants (not all of them tangible, by the way) to those who "honor the Lord" with their finances. In a practical sense, that means giving generously to both improve the lives of those less fortunate and enable those who do not know Christ to hear the good news.

Although Christians have the solemn duty of supporting the ministry of their local church, many find great joy in giving to ministries that accomplish kingdom work that they feel is important. For some, that's feeding the poor. Others financially support efforts to carry the gospel to foreign lands, provide health care to mothers in need, combat human trafficking, or supply clean water to remote villages.

2. Those who make riches their passion lose much more than they gain.
Do not weary yourself to gain wealth,
Cease from your consideration of it.

When you set your eyes on it, it is gone.
For wealth certainly makes itself wings
Like an eagle that flies toward the heavens. (23:4–5)

Who hasn't been tempted by some get-rich-quick scheme? And think of the thousands of people who are drawn into the broad and juicy appeal of investors who promise a killing. Beware of statements like "It's a once-in-a-lifetime opportunity!" and "Get in on the ground floor!" When you hear this kind of stuff, listen for the flapping of eagles' wings and heed instead the wisdom of Solomon's words!

He who tills his land will have plenty of food,
But he who follows empty pursuits will have poverty in plenty.
A faithful man will abound with blessings,
But he who makes haste to be rich will not go unpunished.
A man with an evil eye hastens after wealth
And does not know that want will come upon him. (28:19–20, 22)

Reflections

As you examine your bank records, how much money did you give to your church and meaningful charities in comparison to the amount you spend on entertainment? How much of your discretionary spending can you set aside for giving? If the amount seems insignificant, remember that a single dollar goes a long, long way in underdeveloped countries.

Day 3: *Proverbs 3, 10, 16, 22, 23, 28*
A Difficult Choice

As we continue examining God's money-management princi-ples, we discover a connection between wisdom and wealth.

3. Wisdom gives wealth guidance.

If you have a choice between wisdom and wealth, count on it: wisdom is much to be preferred! With wisdom, you stand a better chance of gaining more wealth, but wealth cannot buy wisdom. And should you be fortunate enough to gain wealth, wisdom will keep you out of trouble.

> Take my instruction and not silver,
> And knowledge rather than choicest gold.
> For wisdom is better than jewels;
> And all desirable things cannot compare with her. . . .
> Riches and honor are with me,
> Enduring wealth and righteousness.
> My fruit is better than gold, even pure gold,
> And my yield better than choicest silver. (8:10–11, 18–19)

> How much better it is to get wisdom than gold!
> And to get understanding is to be chosen above silver. (16:16)

Wisdom provides the recipient of increased finances with the restraint needed to avoid economic disaster. Furthermore, wisdom helps us maintain that essential equilibrium, for much wealth can be a heady trip. In all of human history, riches have never made anyone honest or generous or discerning; wisdom must come aboard to steer our vessel around those dangerous shallow reefs. Which brings us to a fourth principle of money management.

4. Increased riches bring increased complications.

As I examine the biblical record, I find several complications mentioned in the book of Proverbs:

- A false sense of security

The rich man's wealth is his fortress,
The ruin of the poor is their poverty. (10:15)

A rich man's wealth is his strong city,
And like a high wall in his own imagination. (18:11)

- A sudden burst of many new "friends"

He who walks in his uprightness fears the LORD,
But he who is devious in his ways despises Him. (14:2)

A man of too many friends comes to ruin,
But there is a friend who sticks closer than a brother. (18:24)

Wealth adds many friends,
But a poor man is separated from his friend. (19:4)

- The increased probability of arrogance and pride

The poor man utters supplications,
But the rich man answers roughly. (18:23)

The rich man is wise in his own eyes,
But the poor who has understanding sees through him.
(28:11)

- Increased moral temptations

Do not desire her beauty in your heart,
Nor let her capture you with her eyelids.
For on account of a harlot one is reduced to a loaf of bread,
And an adulteress hunts for the precious life.
Can a man take fire in his bosom
And his clothes not be burned?
Or can a man walk on hot coals
And his feet not be scorched? (6:25–28)

A man who loves wisdom makes his father glad,
But he who keeps company with harlots wastes his wealth.
(29:3)

Reflections

If you had the choice between increased wisdom or increased wealth, which would you accept and why? Do your bank statements reflect your choice? What can you do to better align your spending with God's priorities?

Day 4: *Proverbs 3, 10, 16, 22, 23, 28*

The Value of Money

You've probably heard the expression "Money can't buy happiness." Personally, I struggle with that statement because I can think of a lot of things I could buy that would make me very happy! At least for a while. That said, I can also very much affirm—based on personal experience—the absolute validity of the fifth biblical principle concerning money.

5. Money cannot buy life's most valuable possessions.

It is strange how so many people live under the delusion that a fat bank account will make possible the best things in life—when, in fact, it will provide no such thing. Don't misunderstand me. There is nothing wrong with having wealth if you have earned it honestly and if your perspective on your wealth stays solidly biblical. I can affirm the words of vaudeville singer Sophie Tucker, who famously said, "I've been rich and I've been poor—and rich is better."

However, the good life should not be equated with "the true life," which Paul called "life indeed" (1 Timothy 6:19). Money will only buy things that are for sale, and happiness, a clear conscience, and freedom from worry are not! Money can be used to purchase lovely and comfortable dwellings, pleasure vacations, and delightful works of art. But the most valuable things in life are not for sale. What are some of those priceless possessions?

- Peace

Better is a little with the fear of the LORD
Than great treasure and turmoil with it. (15:16)

- Love

Better is a dish of vegetables where love is
Than a fattened ox served with hatred. (15:17)

- A good name, untarnished reputation, and enduring respect

A good name is to be more desired than great wealth,
Favor is better than silver and gold. (22:1)

- Integrity

Better is the poor who walks in his integrity
Than he who is crooked though he be rich. (28:6)

Reflections

At the risk of sounding trite, I'm going to encourage you to take time to count your intangible blessings. Money and possessions aside, what are you truly thankful for? What can you do to increase your intangible assets, such as health, relationships, reputation, contentment, wisdom, etc.?

Day 5: *Proverbs 3, 10, 16, 22, 23, 28*

The Difference Wisdom Makes

On the day before a lottery drawing for more than $600 million, a reporter announced that 40 percent of past lottery grand-prize winners were broke within five years. I was stunned by that figure—I expected it to be higher! That's because I have personally seen this next money-management principle in action.

6. If handled wisely, money can be the means of great en-couragement, but if mishandled, great stress.

Adversity pursues sinners,
But the righteous will be rewarded with prosperity.
A good man leaves an inheritance to his children's children,
And the wealth of the sinner is stored up for the righteous.
(13:21–22)

Many unfortunate lottery winners discover they were not prepared to handle the demands of great wealth. They typically splurged it all away, fell prey to the unwise investment schemes of family and friends, and succumbed to the relentless appeals of charities. A few even committed suicide.

Who can measure the encouragement our money can bring to others? If reared correctly, our children can benefit from, and know the joy of, receiving an inheritance from their parents. God's Word admonishes parents to provide for their families. Ministries of every kind are dependent upon the financial generosity of those who support them. The hungry can be fed, the poor can be clothed, the homeless can be sheltered, the abused can be comforted, the untaught can be educated . . . The list of possibilities is truly endless.

There is the flip side, however:

The rich rules over the poor,
And the borrower becomes the lender's slave.
Do not be among those who give pledges,
Among those who become guarantors for debts.
If you have nothing with which to pay,
Why should he take your bed from under you? (22:7, 26–27)

Pause over those key words . . . especially *slave*. No other term better describes the feeling of being financially irresponsible! If this happens to be your "grind," let me encourage you to ignore it no longer. Make no more excuses! Too many helpful books and reliable resources are available for you. You have no reason to continue in an irresponsible manner. Begin the process of change this week.

Reflections

Several Christian ministries exist to help believers gain wisdom about financial matters. Go online or ask your church about these excellent resources. Don't delay. Regardless of how dire your financial status, it's never too late to start doing what is right.

THE GRIND OF MOTHERHOOD

An excellent wife, who can find?
For her worth is far above jewels.
The heart of her husband trusts in her,
And he will have no lack of gain.
She does him good and not evil
All the days of her life.
She looks for wool and flax
And works with her hands in delight.
She is like merchant ships;
She brings her food from afar.
She rises also while it is still night
And gives food to her household
And portions to her maidens.
She considers a field and buys it;
From her earnings she plants a vineyard.
She girds herself with strength
And makes her arms strong.
She senses that her gain is good;
Her lamp does not go out at night.
She stretches out her hands to the distaff,
And her hands grasp the spindle.
She extends her hand to the poor,
And she stretches out her hands to the needy.
She is not afraid of the snow for her household,
For all her household are clothed with scarlet.
She makes coverings for herself;

Her clothing is fine linen and purple.
Her husband is known in the gates,
When he sits among the elders of the land.
She makes linen garments and sells them,
And supplies belts to the tradesmen.
Strength and dignity are her clothing,
And she smiles at the future.
She opens her mouth in wisdom,
And the teaching of kindness is on her tongue.
She looks well to the ways of her household,
And does not eat the bread of idleness.
Her children rise up and bless her;
Her husband also, and he praises her, saying:
"Many daughters have done nobly,
But you excel them all."
Charm is deceitful and beauty is vain,
But a woman who fears the LORD, she shall be praised.
Give her the product of her hands,
And let her works praise her in the gates.

(Proverbs 31:10–31)

Day 1: *Proverbs 31*

Great Expectations

Without taking away from the joys, rewards, and those ex-tra-special moments of motherhood, I do want to acknowl-edge that the daily tasks of that assignment can be a grind! Washing mounds of laundry; ironing; folding; cleaning; shopping; cooking;

carpooling; being a referee, coach, encourager, counselor, cop; remaining tactful, lovable, compassionate, cheerful, responsible, balanced, and sane (!)—every day, relentlessly repetitive realities like all of these (and there are more!) can make today's mothers feel strung out and spent.

Besides, there is so much for moms to both know and learn. Being a good mother doesn't "just happen" once you have a child. It's as absurd to think that giving birth automatically makes you a good mother as it is to think that having a piano automatically makes you a good musician. An enormous amount of work goes into mothering, more than most people—including many husbands—will ever realize.

Among the eloquent sayings of Scripture is a most outstanding treatise on the mother's role. It is both profound and practical, full of wise counsel and strong encouragement. Anyone who reads this section realizes that God values the woman who gives her home the priority it deserves. He also sees her as a person, distinct and different from her husband, who finds fulfillment in her varied responsibilities and roles.

This week, we will take a close look at someone the wise man Lemuel called "an excellent woman" (Proverbs 31:10).

Reflections

Before we examine the Bible's picture of feminine excellence, consider how your culture defines the ideal woman. What qualities does your society expect in her? How realistic are those standards? How do these standards impact your view of yourself?

Day 2: *Proverbs 31*
Trustworthiness

In the opening lines of his ode to excellent womanhood, Lemuel expressed his great admiration for someone close to him. He obviously wrote from personal observation of someone truly great—perhaps his own wife or mother.

The Hebrew word translated "wife" is the general term for "woman," and the wise man described the excellent woman as a wife and a mother because, in his culture, most women were both. Even so, the character traits he mentioned still apply to all women regardless of their circumstances. The poet's rhetorical question "Who can find?" and his comparison of this woman to a precious stone highlight the fact that a truly excellent woman is indeed rare. A wise husband, therefore, fully appreciates the value of his mate.

> The heart of her husband trusts in her,
> And he will have no lack of gain.
> She does him good and not evil
> All the days of her life.
> Her husband is known in the gates,
> When he sits among the elders of the land.
> Her children rise up and bless her;
> Her husband also, and he praises her, saying:
> "Many daughters have done nobly,
> But you excel them all." (Proverbs 31:11–12, 23, 28–29)

Note the affirmation and respect in those words. There is also supportive companionship between husband and wife: this woman works alongside her man as his faithful partner. He, in turn, praises her publicly and affirms her in private. He makes sure their children appreciate her goodness.

Reflections

The excellent woman is a trustworthy partner in marriage and in business. What do you do in your relationships to cultivate trust? Do your family, friends, and coworkers consider you trustworthy? If you're not certain, ask.

Day 3: *Proverbs 31*

Industriousness

To be honest, I never quite understood the dogmatic assertion, "A woman's place is in the home." While I agree that the responsibility for provision falls upon the man of the house, I see nothing in Scripture that suggests a woman has no part in it. On the contrary, the "excellent woman" of Proverbs 31 is nothing short of a business genius. Far from being cooped up at home and relegated to doing only those restricted tasks, she's in charge of a significant enterprise, overseeing inventory, sales, marketing, employment, distribution, and investment!

Look at the list of her activities mentioned from verses 13–27.

- She looks for good products.
- She works with her hands.
- She invests her wages.
- She makes real estate decisions.
- She provides for herself and her family.
- She runs her own clothing business.
- She even teaches others through her wisdom.

This woman is not simply a drudge: she is an equal partner in every aspect of administering the family's assets. While a husband is responsible for leadership, his responsibility includes supporting his wife's ambitions and helping her reach her full potential. In response, the fulfilled and excellent woman is resourceful, compassionate, strong, and secure. I love the line "She girds herself with strength and makes her arms strong" (v. 17). Only a painfully insecure man wouldn't want this kind of wife.

What a portrait of beauty and strength! Can't you see her smiling as she looks toward the distant horizon of her life? She is neither insecure nor afraid. Her world is bigger than the immediate demands of today. Her strength is an inner strength, a sense of confidence in God. No wonder her children ultimately "bless her"! No wonder her husband happily "praises her"!

Reflections

In what ways can you best support your family and provide for the needs of the household? What talents or skills can you put to good use, not only for the good of your home but also to feel fulfilled? How can you and others in your household work together to help you reach your full potential?

Day 4: *Proverbs 31*

Godly Confidence

The "excellent woman" of Proverbs 31 casts a long shadow for her sisters through history! Not only is she strong, wise, trustworthy, industrious, and successful, but she also "fears the LORD" (v. 30).

The Hebrew word rendered "fear" has a wide range of meanings, including the idea of respectful reverence. I learned about this kind of fear when, fresh out of high school, I began my formal training to become a mechanical engineer. My education included an apprenticeship in a machine shop where I worked with lathes, presses, grinders, and mills, all of them driven by heavy-duty, high-speed motors. I quickly noticed that some of my coworkers had fewer fingers than when they were born. Surprisingly, however, none had suffered a serious injury as a beginner; they lost appendages when they lost their fear of the machines they operated. Lack of reverence for the power of those machines made them complacent and careless.

The "excellent woman" reveres the Lord. She walks with God. She holds Him in highest regard. She maintains a close relationship with the One who gave her life, who maintains her health, cultivates her character, preserves her husband, protects her children, supports her ideas, inspires her creativity, fuels her determination, and blesses her. Consequently, she tackles challenges with confidence. Somehow, you get the impression that this woman doesn't feel like a victim of four walls or a slave to a husband and houseful of kids. She certainly is no social invalid who feels inadequate and overwhelmed. Not in the least! She has found a healthy balance between being herself and remaining extremely involved with, and committed to, her family. She enjoys her husband and the children—and finds other dimensions of fulfillment beyond them.

Reflections

How can a healthy relationship with God fuel your confidence? In what ways can a relationship with God impact your relationships with people? What do you do to cultivate an authentic relationship with the Lord?

Day 5: *Proverbs 31*
Equally Yoked

In 2 Corinthians 6:14 (KJV), Paul the apostle warned believers to avoid being "unequally yoked" with nonbelievers. He used the image of two oxen—one strong, the other weak—harnessed together to pull a plow. Every farmer at the time knew what the outcome would be: the weaker animal invariably set the pace. The stronger animal, trying to remain in step with its partner, will not pull to its full potential.

Issues of salvation aside, the same is true of married partners: inequality of character will limit both people. A lazy husband will tax an industrious woman to destruction. An untrustworthy wife keeps an honest man from finding success. The excellent woman must have an excellent man at her side. He must be incredibly secure and truly generous. He is not only willing to let her find fulfillment beyond him, but he encourages and affirms her doing so. He praises her, openly declaring, "Many daughters have done nobly, but you excel them all" (31:29).

This man is worth a second look, fellow husbands. Maybe it is just male ego on my part, but I am convinced that a significant reason this "excellent wife," who was worth more than precious jewels, found fulfillment in her role as wife, mother, businesswoman, investor, hostess, and friend of the needy was that her husband supported and affirmed those qualities in her. He found delight in her activities. He encouraged her to be the best mother possible, to reach out to others, to become all that God created her to be.

For women who are blessed with a partner like that, motherhood is a glory, not a grind.

Reflections

Take some time for an honest appraisal. If you are a woman, take note of several behind-the-scenes secrets of this woman's life:

- Her positive attitude
- Her indomitable spirit
- Her secure determination
- Her boundless energy
- Her inner strength

If you are a husband, review the comments I made in this last section. Are you a husband worthy of an excellent wife? What can you do to support and encourage your wife to exercise her abilities and find fulfillment using her God-given aspirations?

The Grind of Displeasing God

There are six things which the Lord hates,
Yes, seven which are an abomination to Him:
Haughty eyes, a lying tongue,
And hands that shed innocent blood,
A heart that devises wicked plans,
Feet that run rapidly to evil,
A false witness who utters lies,
And one who spreads strife among brothers.

(Proverbs 6:16–19)

Day 1: *Proverbs 6*
Good Intentions

Even though we have mentioned various aspects of this subject and have glanced at these sayings on more than one occasion in our study together, we need to give them further attention. Who hasn't struggled with the daily grind of displeasing the Lord? Is there a grind that brings greater ache to the soul? None of us begins the day thinking about how we might displease God. On the contrary, most people I know face the dawn with high hopes of pleasing Him. In our minds we establish a game plan that includes a good attitude and wholesome activities. Some people prepare themselves for possible temptations and trials by meeting with God early in the morning and giving Him their day. Yet even when we do so, before the morning is half done, we can behave in ways that are downright discouraging, if not altogether demoralizing.

This week we will focus in on a specific target, on a specific way to please our heavenly Father. Rather than praying in general terms, "Lord, help me to please You," we may benefit more by naming seven specific areas where we need help. This list of seven is inspired—Solomon called them the "seven which are an abomination" to our Lord. At the end of each of the seven discussions that follow, you will find a suggested prayer.

Reflections
What is your primary motivation in wanting to please the Lord? Do you want to please God so life will go well, or do you want to honor the Lord with a good life? Be honest. How will your motivation affect your success?

🔔

Day 2: *Proverbs* 6
Pride and Deception

Solomon's fatherly advice to his son begins with a focus on parts of the body, starting from the head and working down: eyes, tongue, hands, heart, and feet. Today, we take it from the top.

1. Haughty eyes
As the old saying goes, "The eyes are a window to the soul." Did you know that five facial muscles are dedicated to each eye? Those ten muscles serve no other purpose than to express emotion around the eyes. The eyes themselves also help convey so many of

our unspoken feelings or attitudes. Eyes can signal anger, impatience, sorrow, sarcasm, guilt, and especially pride. Naturally, it's this last trait that God finds "abominable."

The Hebrew word for "abomination" refers to anything that God finds personally disgusting. Something that is abominable to God offends His character, and He takes particular exception to it. So what does He find detestable? A "haughty" attitude. The Hebrew means "to be high or elevated," conveying the idea of placing oneself above others, in a position of superiority, and then looking down on them.

God finds this attitude completely absurd. Our universe is measured by eons and light-years so, to the God who created it all, a person standing six feet tall may as well be six millimeters in height. From the vantage point of heaven, the idea of one puny creature looking down on another is laughably repugnant.

Let us all pray, "Lord, reveal to me any hidden arrogance and remove it immediately!"

2. A lying tongue
Elsewhere in the book of Proverbs, the sages wrote,

Lying lips are an abomination to the LORD,
But those who deal faithfully are His delight. (12:22)

Excellent speech is not fitting for a fool,
Much less are lying lips to a prince. (17:7)

Lying takes three primary forms. The first kind is a falsehood about the past: it attempts to recast history in a more favorable light. Not all lies are big and bold. Half-truths and exaggerations definitely qualify as lies. One can also put a spin on past events to highlight favorable details and minimize facts the liar wants overlooked.

The second kind of lie misrepresents the present. Flattery falls into this category. So does insincerity, seduction, or any other attempt to change someone's perception for the purpose of personal gain. Pride also belongs in this grouping, for it is a form of self-deception.

The third lie concerns the future and can take the form of false promises, empty commitments, and signing a contract in bad faith. This kind of lie casts a vision one knows will never transpire.

Because God is truth, lying cannot be more antithetical to His nature. Deception, therefore, is the chief weapon of Satan, the enemy of God and humanity. To lie is to imitate the devil!

Let us pray, "Lord, alert me to the destructive force of my tongue. Keep me from every form of lying!"

Reflections

Pride is notoriously difficult to see in oneself. Ask someone you trust to give you honest feedback. Have that person describe any of your behaviors that communicate the message "I am superior." Then, for the next few days, closely monitor what you say and be on the lookout for any attempt to make what you say more appealing than the reality actually is. Without even realizing it, you may be lying!

Day 3: *Proverbs* 6

Murder and Malice

The Lord's list of abominations—behaviors He intensely detests—continues with the hands and the heart.

3. Hands that shed innocent blood

The *shedding of blood* refers to killing someone, not merely drawing blood in a nonfatal injury, and the qualification "innocent" is important. First, Solomon had murder specifically in mind, an act that the Lord considers an abomination. God created human life, and we bear His image. He considers humanity so valuable that He went to extraordinary lengths to redeem us from evil, sending His Son to die on our behalf. Murder is therefore a personal affront to the Giver of Life.

You might not see right away how this abomination applies to you. Chances are slim you have a body hidden somewhere. The issue for you and me is unresolved anger. Anger itself is not a sin; it's just an emotion. Sometimes resentment is an understandable response when you've been slighted. But if you keep resentment in your clutches, it will destroy you and quite possibly someone else. Nurture your resentment, and it will sprout into anger. That anger will put down deep, deep roots and blossom into hatred, and the fruit of hatred is murder. Don't be fooled. Very few murderers woke up one day and decided to become a killer. I would venture to say that few of them even thought themselves capable of the crime. But by degrees, they nurtured anger until it bore its poisonous fruit in their lives.

Let us pray, "Lord, direct me to wholesome and healthy ways to resolve and dissolve my anger. Keep me from the sin of shedding innocent blood!"

4. A heart that devises wicked plans

We have carefully examined the heart throughout this study of Proverbs, and we are aware of its power. Nothing we do or say occurs unless it first takes root in the heart. It is there that "wicked plans" take shape.

Interestingly, the word *devised* comes from a verb meaning "to plow" and "to engrave." It carries the idea of cutting into some material. A plow cuts into the ground to prepare for planting later, which is an illustration of planning and forethought. The word translated "wicked" means "evil, troublesome, malicious."

God wants the hearts of His people reserved for relationship with Him. He considers the inner being of a person the primary place of worship, a place where we commune with Him. To allow the heart to become a seedbed of evil against others violates a sacred place.

Let us pray, "Lord, cleanse my heart from any hurtful way. Remove every ugly thought or scheme I have been pondering!"

Reflections

Do you have an unresolved conflict with someone, or do you harbor resentment for an offense? Do you ever secretly (or not so secretly) wish that harm would come upon someone you resent? If so, it might be wise to revisit our discussion on "the grind of revenge."

Day 4: *Proverbs 6*

Becoming Numb

Solomon's anatomy of sinful behavior concludes with a look at the evildoer's feet. Not a pretty sight under any circumstances!

5. Feet that run rapidly to evil

This figure of speech actually has more to do with the heart than the feet. First of all, it refers to habitual sin, and old habits are hard to break. Furthermore, because we have gotten away with the sin before, the skids are greased. In fact, we become increasingly brazen and ever less fearful of God's stepping in the longer we walk along those familiar paths to sin. Elsewhere, Solomon writes: "The sentence against an evil deed is not executed quickly, therefore the hearts of the sons of men among them are given fully to do evil" (Ecclesiastes 8:11).

The first instance of sin usually agitates the conscience, prompting repentance. If the repentance is superficial, the second instance of sin becomes less traumatic to our sense of right and wrong. Repeat offenses sear the conscience even further, eventually to the point that it becomes callous, unable to sense the moral impact of a particular deed. That's when we're truly in danger. God made our conscience to respond to His conviction of sin; He considers a seared conscience an abomination.

Let us pray, "God, halt me in my tracks!"

Reflections

Do you engage in any activity you once felt guilty about, but now experience no ill feelings at all? Is there any activity you enjoy that most reasonable people would find immoral? If so, you may need outside help to escape habitual sin and to provide accountability. Don't delay. You're in danger! Confess your sin to a trusted, godly adviser.

Sowers of Dissension

The last two abominations break from the pattern of using body parts as illustrations. The Lord finds these activities detestable, and they are linked together because they have similar effects on the community of God's people.

6. *A false witness who utters lies*

Rare are the truth tellers, and many are those who deliberately misrepresent the facts. When we have the opportunity to defend another's character or set the record straight among those who are bad-mouthing a certain individual, the temptation is great to either chime in and agree or remain silent and allow the character assassination to continue. But the Lord *hates* such actions. As we discussed earlier, God's character is truth. Deception is the favorite tool of Satan, who loves nothing more than to drive God's people apart. When we lie, we side with the devil against God and His people.

Let us pray, "Lord, free me from whatever fears I have so that my witness will be true, based on accurate facts!"

7. *One who spreads strife among brothers*

When two people experience a conflict, we have a choice to make. We can reinforce the division, or we can encourage reconciliation. Anything we say regarding their dispute will accomplish one or the other. Furthermore, we can also use that opportunity to pull the community together or to encourage members to take sides. Again, anything we say to others about the matter will accomplish one or the other.

Observe how Paul the apostle discussed a dispute in an open letter to the community of believers in Philippi:

I urge Euodia and I urge Syntyche to live in harmony in the Lord. Indeed, true companion, I ask you also to help these women who have shared my struggle in the cause of the gospel, together with Clement also and the rest of my fellow workers, whose names are in the book of life.

Rejoice in the Lord always; again I will say, rejoice! Let your gentle spirit be known to all men. The Lord is near. Be anxious for nothing, but in everything by prayer and supplication with thanksgiving let your requests be made known to God. And the peace of God, which surpasses all comprehension, will guard your hearts and your minds in Christ Jesus.

Finally, brethren, whatever is true, whatever is honorable, whatever is right, whatever is pure, whatever is lovely, whatever is of good repute, if there is any excellence and if anything worthy of praise, dwell on these things. The things you have learned and received and heard and seen in me, practice these things, and the God of peace will be with you. (Philippians 4:2–9)

Note that Paul did not take sides or encourage their community to become polarized by the dispute. Paul had them focus on Christ, on God's faithfulness, on the beauty of the gospel, and on their common bond in the kingdom of God. He intended his every word to restore unity rather than perpetuate strife.

Let us pray, "Lord, make me a peacemaker."

We may frequently think about the love of God, but all too seldom do we meditate on the things He hates. We should! Believe me, we need to pay attention when God's Word says He hates these things. Our efforts to correct and control each abomination need to be as intense as His abhorrence of them.

Reflections

How can you encourage greater unity in your family, your neighborhood, your workplace, and your church? Obviously, you can't fix other people's problems, but you can keep yourself from becoming a part of them. Without becoming meddlesome, what can you do to encourage healthy communication between others?

THE GRIND OF SUBSTITUTING KNOWLEDGE FOR WISDOM

The proverbs of Solomon the son of David, king of Israel:

To know wisdom and instruction,
To discern the sayings of understanding,
To receive instruction in wise behavior,
Righteousness, justice and equity;
To give prudence to the naive,
To the youth knowledge and discretion,
A wise man will hear and increase in learning,
And a man of understanding will acquire wise counsel,
To understand a proverb and a figure,
The words of the wise and their riddles.

The fear of the LORD is the beginning of knowledge;
Fools despise wisdom and instruction.

Hear, my son, your father's instruction
And do not forsake your mother's teaching;
Indeed, they are a graceful wreath to your head
And ornaments about your neck.
My son, if sinners entice you,
Do not consent.
If they say, "Come with us,
Let us lie in wait for blood,
Let us ambush the innocent without cause;

Let us swallow them alive like Sheol,
Even whole, as those who go down to the pit;
We will find all kinds of precious wealth,
We will fill our houses with spoil;
Throw in your lot with us,
We shall all have one purse,"
My son, do not walk in the way with them.
Keep your feet from their path,
For their feet run to evil
And they hasten to shed blood.
Indeed, it is useless to spread the baited net
In the sight of any bird;
But they lie in wait for their own blood;
They ambush their own lives.
So are the ways of everyone who gains by violence;
It takes away the life of its possessors.

Wisdom shouts in the street,
She lifts her voice in the square;
At the head of the noisy streets she cries out;
At the entrance of the gates in the city she utters her sayings:
"How long, O naive ones, will you love being simple-minded?
And scoffers delight themselves in scoffing
And fools hate knowledge?
"Turn to my reproof,
Behold, I will pour out my spirit on you;
I will make my words known to you."

(Proverbs 1:1–23)

Day 1: *Proverbs 1*
Knowledge versus Wisdom

When we first looked at the sayings of Solomon and the wise men of Israel, we began with Proverbs 1. It occurs to me that it would be worthwhile to return to it as we consider for the final time our tendency to substitute knowledge for wisdom. This is not only a daily grind; it is a lifetime challenge!

How easy it is to acquire knowledge, yet how difficult and painstaking is the process of gaining wisdom. Man shares knowledge; God gives wisdom. Knowledge comes as we get an education, either by absorbing what the highly educated have to say or by simply gathering information here and there along life's road. But what about the wisdom that is from above? As you already know, there is no course, no school, no earthly data bank where divine wisdom can be accessed. And unlike knowledge, which can be measured in objective analyses, quantified by exams, and certified by diplomas and degrees, wisdom defies measurement; it is much more subjective, takes far more time to acquire, and has a great deal to do with our attitude. One can be knowledgeable, yet distant from the living God. But those who are wise know the Lord God by faith in His Son, Jesus Christ, and they also hold Him in awe and respect. "Fear of the Lord" is still the beginning of wisdom as well as the truest indicator of its presence in a person.

So how does one obtain wisdom? And now that we have come to the end of our search through the sayings of Israel's wisest men, how can we continue our pursuit of God's wisdom? Also, what are some ways to guard against falling back into our habit of substituting knowledge for wisdom?

I have four suggestions. We'll examine them individually over the next four days.

Based on all we have studied together, explain your understanding of the difference between knowledge and wisdom. What is the potential danger of having knowledge without wisdom?

Day 2: *Proverbs 1*

An Annual Refresher Course

We have given much thought to the subject of wisdom and taken time to hear the counsel of ancient Israel's wisest teachers. This discipline undoubtedly supplied you with lots of helpful information. Such knowledge is a good beginning, but I hope you won't be satisfied with mere knowledge of the Bible. My first suggestion for becoming wise might seem obvious or maybe even redundant. Nevertheless, I stand by it.

1. Read the book of Proverbs regularly.

The proverbs of Solomon the son of David, king of Israel:
To know wisdom and instruction,
To discern the sayings of understanding,
To receive instruction in wise behavior,
Righteousness, justice and equity;
To give prudence to the naive,
To the youth knowledge and discretion,
A wise man will hear and increase in learning,
And a man of understanding will acquire wise counsel,
To understand a proverb and a figure,
The words of the wise and their riddles.

The fear of the LORD is the beginning of knowledge;
Fools despise wisdom and instruction. (1:1–7)

The book of Proverbs has thirty-one chapters, making it a nice fit for a monthly read-through. You can read a chapter each day in a typical month. There is no mumbo jumbo, no complex theology to unscramble, no abstract theories to unravel. Proverbs is straight talk for all of us who live imperfect lives on planet earth. Furthermore, since Solomon declared that his writings have been recorded to help us "know wisdom," I suggest we take him up on it and glean new dimensions of wisdom by sitting at his feet.

Read Proverbs regularly and often, but don't merely review the information. Apply the principles and observe their impact on your life as you live them out. Most importantly, read prayerfully. Ask God to reveal mysteries to you through the ministry of His Holy Spirit. Ask Him to reveal yourself to you. As you discover your own sinfulness, shortcomings, woundedness, and spiritual needs, ask for His guidance and healing. As time passes and the Spirit of God applies His Word, you *will* become increasingly wise.

Reflections

Set aside at least one month each year (once every six months is better) to read a chapter of Proverbs each day and make this a life-long practice. I recommend January and July. Each has thirty-one days. They're six months apart. And a reminder of the truth of Proverbs in January would be a perfect way to start off each new year.

Seasoned Citizens of the Kingdom

No source of wisdom can match the timeless, infallible, inerrant Word of God. But don't ignore the wisdom of other seasoned believers.

2. Hear and heed the counsel of those you respect.

Hear, my son, your father's instruction
And do not forsake your mother's teaching;
Indeed, they are a graceful wreath to your head
And ornaments about your neck. (1:8–9)

While the Bible is our only source of infallible, inerrant wisdom, it is not our only source of godly counsel. God has given you godly women and men in the community of Christ's body, the church. Seasoned Christian mentors have been through some experiences and endured some trials that you have not yet encountered. They have had time to weave their failures and successes through their study of the Scriptures, and their experience gives them a discernment and depth you may yet lack. The things they can pass along to you are "a graceful wreath" and "ornaments" of wisdom. Listen to these wise believers. Learn from them. Linger with them.

Reflections

Think of a seasoned believer in Jesus Christ, preferably of the same gender, whom you respect and trust. Offer to treat that person to lunch, dinner, or coffee—once a week indefinitely. Explain your desire to ask questions and to hear about their spiritual growth.

Day 4: *Proverbs 1*
Keeping Good Company

In our continuing quest for divine wisdom, I have suggested, first, that we read Proverbs regularly and, second, that we gain the perspective of experienced, godly believers. We must also guard what we have.

3. Choose your friends carefully.

My son, if sinners entice you,
Do not consent.
If they say, "Come with us,
Let us lie in wait for blood,
Let us ambush the innocent without cause;
Let us swallow them alive like Sheol,
Even whole, as those who go down to the pit;
We will find all kinds of precious wealth,
We will fill our houses with spoil;
Throw in your lot with us,
We shall all have one purse,"
My son, do not walk in the way with them.
Keep your feet from their path,
For their feet run to evil
And they hasten to shed blood.
Indeed, it is useless to spread the baited net
In the sight of any bird;
But they lie in wait for their own blood;
They ambush their own lives.

So are the ways of everyone who gains by violence;
It takes away the life of its possessors. (1:10–19)

The longer I live, the more careful I am with my choice of friends. Don't get me wrong. I will offer my support and friendship to almost anyone. I am, however, choosy about whom I accept as close confidants, those people I allow to minister *to me*. And, because my time is precious, I elect to spend it with trustworthy people. Consequently, I have fewer close friends than I had in my youth. But these are deeper friendships, truly treasured relationships.

As Solomon counseled us, do not consent to relationships that drag you down, interfere with your walk with God, or hinder your spiritual growth. Offer your friendship freely to those you hope to influence, but avoid people who "ambush their own lives" (v. 18). They will not be influenced; they will simply get you involved in counterproductive activities that keep wisdom at arm's distance. You don't need that. No one does.

Reflections

What are some relationships from which you might need to withdraw, at least for a season? What are some relationships you would like to cultivate? Think of some ways you can involve yourself with other wise people you admire.

Day 5: *Proverbs 1*
The School of Hard Knocks

Consistent interaction with God's Word, regular time spent with a godly mentor, and a choice group of friends all combine to give us the greatest opportunity for growth in wisdom. To these, I would add one more suggestion.

4. Pay close attention to life's reproofs.

Wisdom shouts in the street,
She lifts her voice in the square;
At the head of the noisy streets she cries out;
At the entrance of the gates in the city she utters her sayings:
"How long, O naive ones, will you love being simple-minded?
And scoffers delight themselves in scoffing
And fools hate knowledge?
Turn to my reproof,
Behold, I will pour out my spirit on you;
I will make my words known to you." (1:20–23)

If you have been on this journey through the Proverbs for the last six months, perhaps you recall the time we spent studying these lines. Wisdom is personified as one who "shouts in the street" and "lifts her voice in the square." In other words, she doesn't hide; she's easily found. She doesn't whisper or garble her words; she speaks loud and clear. But where? And how? She tells us when she says, "Turn to my reproof." In life's reproofs wisdom shouts in our ears. God sends Lady Wisdom at the right time and with the right message when we are most apt to listen: after we fail at something.

God never wastes our time. He doesn't allow us to go through dark and dismal valleys or endure those long, winding, and painful paths for no reason. In each one are "reproofs" with wisdom attached. Many and foolish are those who simply grit their teeth and bear life's hard times. Few but wise are those who hear wisdom's voice and listen to her counsel.

Failures and foibles can become our greatest opportunities to grow in wisdom. Remain ever watchful for reproofs and never discount their source. God's reproving wisdom comes through the most unlikely means sometimes. Lessons will be obvious if we're not blinded by our pride. Watch for them. Listen carefully. Heed the voice of wisdom.

Reflections

Try to remember your last significant failure. Think carefully about the aftermath. Did someone or something offer a reproof? Did you miss it? Or did you notice the reproof but decide to ignore it? How, if at all, did the reproof increase your wisdom? How will you respond after your next significant failure?

ABOUT THE AUTHOR

Charles R. Swindoll has devoted over four decades to two passions: an unwavering commitment to the practical communication and application of God's Word, and an untiring devotion to seeing lives transformed by God's grace. Chuck graduated *magna cum laude* from Dallas Theological Seminary and has since been honored with four doctorates. For his teaching on *Insight for Living*, he has received the Program of the Year award and the Hall of Fame award from the National Religious Broadcasters, as well as multiple book awards. He and his wife of over half a century, Cynthia, live in Texas. You can find out more about Chuck at www.insight.org.

WORTHY

PUBLISHING

IF YOU LIKED THIS BOOK . . .

- Tell your friends by going to: www.livingtheproverbs.net and clicking "LIKE"

- Head over to the facebook.com/worthypublishing page, click "LIKE" and post a comment regarding what you enjoyed about the book

- Tweet "I recommend reading #LivingtheProverbs by @CharlesSwindoll // @Worthypub"

- Hashtag: #LivingtheProverbs

- Subscribe to our newsletter by going to www.worthy publishing.com

WORTHY PUBLISHING
FACEBOOK PAGE

WORTHY PUBLISHING
WEBSITE